Advanced STAMP COLLECTING

*A Serious Collector's Guide to the
Collection and Study of
Postage Stamps and Related Materials*

Barry Krause

BETTERWAY PUBLICATIONS, INC.
WHITE HALL, VIRGINIA

Published by Betterway Publications, Inc.
P.O. Box 219
Crozet, VA 22932
(804) 823-5661

Cover design by Susan Riley
Typography by Park Lane Associates

Library of Congress Cataloging-in-Publication Data

Krause, Barry
   Advanced stamp collecting : a serious collector's guide to the
collection and study of postage stamps and related materials / by
Barry Krause.
     p. cm.
   Includes bibliographical references and index.
   ISBN 1-55870-159-1 (pbk.) : $9.95
1. Postage-stamps--Collectors and collecting. I. Title.
HE6213.K68 1990
769.56--dc20   90-39099
                                          CIP

Printed in the United States of America
0 9 8 7 6 5 4 3 2 1

LETTERS

Every day brings a ship,
Every ship brings a word;
Well for those who have no fear,
Looking seaward well assured
That the word the vessel brings
Is the word they wish to hear.

Ralph Waldo Emerson (1867)

ACKNOWLEDGMENTS

The stamp dealers in Chapter 7 — who shared their time and knowledge with me.

The museums and libraries in Chapter 10 — who gave me information about their organizations.

The staff of Santa Monica Public Library, Santa Monica, CA — for helping me with research.

KODALUX Processing Services of Hollywood, CA and Palo Alto, CA — for film developing of the photo negatives.

Richard Photo Lab of Los Angeles, CA — for printing the prints from the negatives.

Collectors and dealers — who supported my first two philatelic books: *Collecting Stamps for Pleasure & Profit* and *Stamp Collecting: An Illustrated Guide and Handbook for Adult Collectors* (both by Betterway Publications, Inc.).

The loyal readers of my column "Your Stamps," which has appeared in the *Los Angeles Times* since 1982.

Stamp Collector newspaper of Albany, OR — for allowing me to quote three paragraphs from my former column, "Collectively Speaking," which appeared in the May 6, 1978 issue of *Stamp Collector,* page 13.

Federal Express — for carrying the manuscript.

The U.S. Postal Service (and its predecessor, the U.S. Post Office Department) — for making the stamps that I write about.

The staff of Betterway Publications, Inc., especially Robert F. Hostage and Hilary W. Swinson — for superb editing of the raw manuscripts that I send to them.

ABOUT THE STAMPS ON THE FRONT COVER

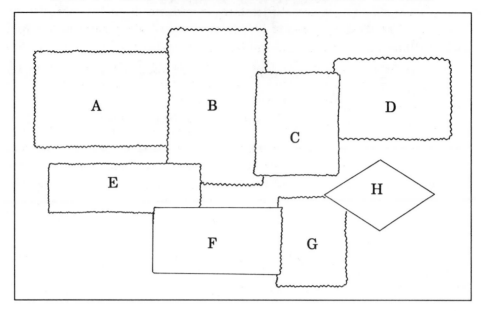

A. 50¢ Graf Zeppelin U.S. air mail block-of-four cancelled with a first day of issue New York, N.Y. circular date stamp of Oct. 2, 1933. Well-centered, undamaged used block (many of them are not). Rare when cancelled for commercial non-Zeppelin usage.

B. Unused pair of Mount Everest Expedition local label of 1924. Printed in panes of 36 with selvage all around. Comes in various shades of blue. Often without gum or regummed. Usually off center. Was used on 1924 Mount Everest expedition post cards, which are usually found defective with corner bends, creases, surface scrapes.

C. New Zealand Antarctic Expedition mint block-of-four issued for the 1911 Scott Expedition, overprinted "VICTORIA LAND." Use a ten-power (or stronger) magnifier to see the *comma* instead of the *period* after the word "LAND" on the lower left stamp. Rare with no stop at all after LAND; beware of fraudently removed stops. Unlisted in American catalogs.

D. $1 Trans-Mississippi Exposition commemorative (Western Cattle in Storm) issued June 17, 1898. Lightly cancelled used copy, well centered, and with *no defects* (top perforations have been trimmed off in the photograph). Scarce in truly undamaged condition, either mint or used.

E. Transvaal 2-shillings Queen Victoria issue of 1878 in strip of four, cancelled Pretoria, August, 1883. Rare in multiples or on cover. The entire set of seven values of this 1878-80 Victoria issue is usually found off center with poor margins. Missing perfs common. Lower values are scarce in full panes. British auction companies overgrade this set in catalog descriptions ("superb used" means something extraordinary in America).

F. 4¢ Trans-Mississippi Exposition issue: "INDIAN HUNTING BUF-FALO" cancelled on piece at Pittsburg (notice no "h" at the end), PA on Oct. 9, 1899. Tied on piece at left straight edge. Many normal straight edges from panes of U.S. Columbian or Trans-Mississippi stmaps have been perforated to increase their market value. First issued June 17, 1898, a first-day cover of this 4¢ stamp would command several thousand dollars at auction (if in nice condition).

G. 2¢ Black Jack definitive of July 1863. Design is clear of all perforations, better than average. With *pen cancel* expertly removed. Superb copies of the Black Jack with large, even margins and no defects are almost nonexistent. Auction catalog describers notoriously overgrade this stamp; there aren't many truly "extremely fine" Black Jacks. How would you grade the centering of the Black Jack on this book's cover?

H. California Bicycle Mail local of 1894 with retouched die (San Francisco spelling error corrected). Mint, gummed, this variety is worth about $15 as a single; properly tied on a pristine cover of this mail service it approaches $1000 market value. Established by Arthur C. Banta (Fresno, CA agent for Victor Bicycles), this local post lasted about two weeks in July 1894, with bicycle messengers carrying letters between Fresno and San Francisco during the American Railway Union strike. These local post stamps were used on covers also franked with U.S. government postage.

Contents

Introduction

In his article "Stamp Collecting" in the *Bulletin of the Menninger Clinic* (Vol. 6, No. 3, May 1942, pp. 71-74), William C. Menninger, M.D. says that he started collecting stamps at about age eight, probably by imitating his older brothers. He further goes on to analyze the psychology of collecting, a striving for systematic order in life by the search for, and the subsequent arrangement of, acquisitions: "Stamp collecting thus furnishes ideal outlets for compulsive activity."

And although few collectors would care to delve so deeply into their motives, Otto Fenichel in his article "The Drive to Amass Wealth" (*The Psychoanalytic Quarterly*, Vol. VII, No. 1, Jan. 1938, pp. 69-95) points out that the desire to own things and keep them forever has roots in our protection and preservation of our own selves: "In the deeper layers of the mind, the idea of possessions refers to the contents of one's own body, which could be taken away."

Whatever the reasons, stamp collecting for many people has an attraction and fascination far beyond the appeal of most non-essential human activities. There is some truth in admitting that you are "addicted" to philately, and those of us who have spent many pleasant hours with stamps will plead guilty with pride when accused of being obsessed with stamp collecting!

This book isn't a substitute for the numerous learned treatises on philatelic specialties; nor is it all-encompassing in even the subjects that it covers. "Advanced" collecting is a state of mind as well as a group of objective achievements (exhibiting, winning awards, writing stamp articles, amassing the "finest" collection of its type, etc.). There are degrees of "advancement," and the prudent philatelist is ever eager to learn from and absorb the knowledge of others.

Stamps are a window to the past, a paper link between living and past generations, a documentary record of the glory and foibles of human beings. Curiosity and wonder propel the dedicated philatelist into ever-expanding areas of research, into unanticipated backroads of postal history, into thrilling encounters with real and imagined stamp dilemmas. Who but a stamp collector gets excited when glancing at a faded postmark or when discovering for the first time a previously unrecognized rarity?

Stamp collecting leads us to new friends and acquaintances, some of whom we might only know from extended mail correspondence. Stamp collecting makes us pay meticulous attention to detail, a trait of incalculable benefit in other life pursuits. Stamps refresh our memories about geography, history, politics, economics, art, and human nature; the very birth and death of nations and nations' leaders can be demonstrated in the pageant of the world's postage stamps of the last century.

Philately is a respectable hobby, and often profitable financially and professionally (for diligent dealers and lucky investors). Stamps provide escape and relaxation from stressful daily affairs.

The easiest thing in the world is to criticize. Clifford T. Morgan, in his article "The Hoarding Instinct" (*Psychological Review,* Vol. 54, No. 6, Nov. 1947) writes: "Men sometimes spend their lives accumulating vast hoards of wealth and property which they can never use. Some simply collect more or less useless objects — jewelry, antiques, glassware, stamps . . . " (p. 335)

But I view stamps as a positive force in the lives of those who bother to investigate and study these little bits of historical paper. In my former column "Collectively Speaking" in *Stamp Collector* newspaper, I once had an article entitled "Instead of a psychiatrist, see your stamp album" (May 6, 1978 issue, page 13). I concluded by saying:

"Spend 10 or 15 minutes with your favorite stamp or cover. Study its features all over again. Look for something in it that you've never seen before. Remember where and when you obtained it, and how happy you were to own it.

"Visit a psychiatrist if you must. Read the latest psychology paperbacks if you need to. Worry a lot and get depressed if you feel it is necessary.

"But please don't forget your stamps. They need you as much as you need them."

Chapter 1

Collecting Goals

You're going to live in the future, so you should plan for it. You don't have to act out all of the details of your life according to an encyclopedic script, but it is amazing how few people bother to write down some simple goals that they wish to achieve — with a few remarks about how they intend to accomplish their objectives. Hazy fantasies pondered in your mind may remain there unless you start making them a reality by writing them down and analyzing their assets and liabilities, and *then* taking actual steps to reach such goals.

PLANNING A COLLECTION There are four main purposes in assembling a quality stamp collection: research, investment, exhibition, and personal satisfaction. A collection may have one of these goals as its overriding purpose, or some combination of them with no primary emphasis. To make good use of your time and efforts, you have to decide on your collecting goals.

Research *Research* and its resulting knowledge are the driving forces that expand the intense curiosity of a serious philatelist. It isn't enough merely to accumulate and mount stamps; we have to *learn* about them and do in-depth research to explore (but never exhaust) the mysteries behind each stamp that touches our tongs.

It was the brilliant research of scholars like Stanley B. Ashbrook, Lester G. Brookman, Dr. Carroll Chase, and John N. Luff that set the standard by which original philatelic investigations are conducted. If a major goal of your collection is original research, you must first read everything that has been published on your specialty (including other languages if possible), then define your research goals with an eye to the prospects of their reasonable accomplishment in your lifetime with your available funds.

Examples of long-term research projects in U.S. philately would be: (1) Printing Varieties of the 2¢ Black Jack (including grills, different papers, inks, double transfers, plate characteristics, and production errors); (2) Foreign Mail Usage of the 1901 Pan-American Series; (3) Domestic Cancels on the Parcel Post Stamps During the Year 1913; and (4) Essays and Proofs of U.S. Postage Dues. The last choice would be expensive, and all of these projects would require many years of searching for any hope of relative "completeness."

Costs *Costs* limit the depth of self-acquired stamps for research. If you are going to buy the stamps that you study (rather than use someone else's collection or museum specimens), then you have to draw up a list of costs that you anticipate spending to achieve your research goals. If you are going to reconstruct sheets of un-used, undamaged four-margined Penny Blacks, then you need a big wallet. If funds are quite limited, then select a collecting specialty that matches your budget, like common World War II U.S. patriotic covers or cancelled Canadian air post issues.

INVESTMENT If *investment* is your major collecting goal, choose stamps with a good potential for future price appreciation. You may not be interested in a stamp's background, or even like its design, but you should buy it if it fits your long-term investment goals. While philatelic research dictates studying the same stamp varieties, investment requires diversity to spread the financial risk over many different issues.

Pick stamps with a good track record in market price increases (like VF-XF sound 19th century U.S.), stick with one or two favorite countries so you know what you're buying, go for top condition consistent with fair prices (damaged stamps make skeptical buyers), and think expensive for serious investing (buy one stamp at $100 rather than ten stamps at $10 each). Keep *records* of all stamp investments including date purchased, amount paid, source (dealer, auction, etc.), and condition. Enter the information on file cards or in a computer inventory. Two companies that sell software for inventorying stamp collections are:

Inventory

DGS Systems
33 Ticonderoga
Millis, MA 02054
(508) 376-5783

Compu-Quote
6914 Berquist Avenue
Canoga Park, CA 91307
(818) 348-3662, Ext. 11

Typical software programs for stamp collection inventory run a little less than $100 each, and are well worth the expense if you have a computer and are spending a lot of money for stamp investment.

And stamp investments should be made with surplus funds (*not* the rent or car payment money). Buy with expertizing certificates for items about which you have doubts; deal with reliable, established dealers; buy expensive stamps with low press runs; and stick with quality rather than quantity for maximum profits.

If you want to know what I would buy for long-term (ten years or more) investment, how about: VF-XF 19th century mint and used U.S. (*undamaged*), pre-World War II U.S. air mails in plate blocks, early Great Britain imperf. line engraved issues with large margins, Wells, Fargo covers costing over $100 each, U.S. Columbian and Trans-Mississippian stamps without defects, Zeppelin stamps and covers of the world, U.S. Civil War patriotic covers costing over $100 each, major Scott listed errors, encased postage stamps, and anything expensive (over $100) from the Confederate States of America, Hawaii, or Guam overprints.

EXHIBITING

Exhibition requires careful planning, endless effort, and sometimes a large bankroll if you seek gold medal-winning stamp exhibits. If your collecting goal is to assemble a meaningful set of exhibition-quality album pages, then you need precise strategies of attack if you have any hope of accomplishing your dreams.

Will you live long enough to complete an exhibit of elusive material, do you have enough money, and can you find the information necessary to write up your stamps? In Chapter 6 we'll look at the crucial aspects of competitive philatelic exhibiting.

PERSONAL SATISFACTION

Personal satisfaction is a subjective, intangible reward that can only be judged by the individual collector involved. We collect things for many emotional reasons, including the acquiring of a sense of control over our lives via the collection and arrangement of small objects.

We collect to show our treasure to friends and strangers; to experience the thrill of the chase in tracking down and recognizing choice additions to our collections. When you finally hinge that last stamp of a rare set, or discover a previously "unknown" variety of cancellation, then you feel the wonder and joy that explorers in all ages have felt.

An advanced philatelist may never exhibit, never spend over $100 for a stamp, and may not care at all for the investment aspect of his collection. But he may still lose himself in the research, pleasure, and intense investigation of philatelic problems — as much as those people who sport a display case full of exhibit medals or a portfolio brimming with Confederate Provisionals.

COMPLETENESS

Completeness is relative. Some advanced U.S. collectors consider their albums complete if they obtain one example of each of the major Scott listed numbers. Other collectors feel they need all major varieties and shades for a "complete" collection. You must define your long-term collecting goals and decide as you work towards them whether completeness is affordable, obtainable, or even desirable for your collecting specialty.

For example, what is a complete collection of U.S. Columbian commemoratives of 1893? A mint and used single of each denomination? Plus margin imprint and plate number blocks of six? Plus on cover usages, including first-days and Exposition station cancels? Plus imperf. pairs, multiple transfers, and other plate flaws?

Do you have a "complete" set of Columbians if you lack the Proofs? The China and Supplementary Mail cancels? Should you get full panes of fifty (where available!) and cancelled blocks of four to be complete? Commercial and philatelically-inspired covers, overseas usage, and mixed franking Columbian covers? Do you need artists' drawings and other collateral to have a complete representation of this stamp set? Maybe for an International Gold Medal Collection; maybe not for the collecting purposes of lesser mortals!

In my opinion, the best collection is the one that is never finished, that is always being worked on, that inspires and fascinates its owner with new discoveries made periodically. Completeness is a state of mind more than it is an objective standard in philatelic achievement. In exhibiting, for example, the *title* of the collection defines and limits the boundaries of the material presented, and reasonable judges evaluate stamp exhibits accordingly. Don't long for completeness in a collection of 19th

Century German States unless you have a deep wallet (and the ability to detect early German forgeries). There is nothing wrong with narrowing the scope and title of your collection to make it more manageable.

CONDITION

Condition makes or breaks a potential prize-winning collection. Exhibitors follow the well-known rule that they should strive to obtain stamps in the best *available* condition. Most Boer War prisoner-of-war covers have slight defects, and an exhibit of such covers in pristine condition would be truly impressive (no envelope creases or stains, the adhesive stamps "perfectly centered," clear bold cancellation strikes, etc.). The 1938 U.S. Presidential definitives are modern enough that nice copies, mint or used, are readily found, so a detailed study of the Presidentials in lousy condition would be laughable.

Depending on the material, a sensible stamp investment portfolio should contain VF or better items by *objective* standards (i.e., with even balanced margins, no perf. defects, clean cancels), and *not* VF "for the year of issue." When contemplating the purchase of a stamp for investment, its condition should make it stand out in its own right when compared with "normal" copies of that issue. Well-centered dollar-value Columbians ($1-$5 issues) and Trans-Mississippians ($1-$2) with no visible defects (under 10 power magnification, *and* under ultraviolet examination, *and* in watermark fluid), either mint or used, are prime investment choices. You get what you pay for in stamps; there should be nothing about an investment stamp that bothers you. If there is, don't buy it, because that real or imagined defect will probably bother the next buyer also.

When flipping through an auction catalog or wandering along table displays at bourses and shows, be alert for stamps that seem to say "Buy Me!" You undoubtedly will pay more, but you'll be proud to own them. I've never regretted buying an expensive stamp; it is easy to resell, it is easy to use as collateral for a loan, and everybody else who sees it likes it too! Keep it for twenty years and then throw it in an auction and watch what happens.

FINDING STAMPS

Finding stamps can be difficult if they are extremely scarce and seldom come up at auction. You expect to see sets of the 1930 Zeppelins in every large U.S. stamp auction; these stamps are valuable but not particularly scarce. You don't expect to see proofs and essays of mid-20th century U.S. commemoratives —

these are rather hard to find, and definitely underpriced in the Scott catalog because there is much less demand for such items than for mint Zeppelin sets.

Get on the mailing lists of important dealers who stock your collecting specialty (see Chapters 7 and 8). *Always* visit stamp shops when in a strange city. They're listed in the Yellow Pages of the Telephone book in your hotel or motel room. If necessary, as some advanced philatelists do, you can even run regular classified ads in the stamp periodicals, offering to buy items such as hometown covers, Sanitary Fairs, or Greek Hermes heads. Obviously you must establish financial trust when you deal with the general public via classified.

If your research shows that such stamps once existed and may still exist, then you have a lifelong search cut out for you in locating these things. I felt vicarious excitement at a stamp show in San Francisco when Joe Rourke, the former Black Jack specialist, walked up to a relatively unaffluent cover dealer's table and asked to see his Black Jack covers. Then, when Mr. Rourke shuffled through the few covers that he was handed, I peered over his shoulder and wondered what his expert eyes were seeing that I was missing!

If necessary, you may have to travel to a foreign country to see dealers who have items in your specialty, or get specialist approvals mailed to you from faraway dealers.

COLLECTION COHERENCE

Is your collection coherent? Does it tell a logical story? Do all of your items make sense in chronological and philatelic sequence? Are there any inexcusable gaps in your exhibit?

Suppose you wanted to document the production and usages of the 50¢ "Baby" Zeppelin of 1933. Some proofs and essays are in order (beware of forged "photo" essays which I saw offered at auction a few years ago), and original artists' sketches if you can find them. Then a full mint pane of fifty in a single exhibit frame. Then mint and used singles, annotated printing errors (quite scarce), and a nice selection of covers (including first days from *all* the cities: New York, Akron, Washington, Miami, and Chicago) with domestic and international destinations. Try to locate a commercial *non-philatelic* 50¢ Zeppelin cover of that time period if you want something truly rare. Finally, a little Zeppelin collateral might round out your collection: pieces of the actual airship, original photographs of its exterior and interior, and signed letters or other documents related to its flights (how about an ALS [autograph letter signed] by the Zeppelin's captain, commenting on the joys and pains of carrying mail on board his airship?).

A collection that is "complete," coherent, and well-organized with top quality material is a treasure to behold, and worthy of inclusion in serious stamp exhibitions.

Chapter 2

Mailing Rates and Postal History

Nineteenth century U.S. letter rates for domestic mail of the adhesive stamp era, selected first-day cover dates, Territorial and Statehood dates, and the dates of certain U.S. mail service innovations are all discussed in this chapter, with explanatory tables. The serious philatelist knows that knowledge is strength, and a familiarity with (or even partial memorization of) the known data of postal history will not disappoint the person making the effort.

You may never make the longed-for "find" of a rare FDC or pre-Statehood cover in a bourse dealer's junk box, but it pays to know some basic dates and rates that apply to your collecting specialty so that you can verify the apparent authenticity of a cancel or cover. I concentrated on 19th century information because 20th century rates are better known, simpler, or less crucial (in monetary value or philatelic significance).

19TH CENTURY LETTER RATES The 19th century U.S. *letter rates* cited are for what is now called "first class" mail, i.e., written personal or business letters sent at the most expeditious routings without resorting to special delivery type services. My table only indicates domestic mail — letters sent from and to a United States post office. Foreign mail rates are a philatelic nightmare in the mid-19th century, and these are best left for referral to books such as: Charles J. Starnes, *United States Letter Rates to Foreign Destinations 1847 to GPU-UPU.* (Leonard H. Hartmann, Louisville, KY, 1982.) When Starnes' book was published, I loaned my copy to postal rate expert Henry W. Beecher of Ashland, OR, who returned the book with a detailed single-spaced five-page typed letter (dated August 26, 1982) in which he gives his opinions on some aspects of the book! Such is the willingness of postal historians to share their knowledge unselfishly and liberally.

But regarding the table of letter rates, you must remember that a given cover may not seem to "fit" the rates quoted for its time period because (1) it is overweight (or was, when it was mailed);

UNITED STATES FIRST CLASS RATES WITHIN THE COUNTRY		
Date Effective	**Distances**	**Prepaid Rates**
July 1, 1845	Less than 300 miles More than 300 miles Local Drop Letters	5¢ per half ounce 10¢ per half ounce 2¢
1847	Between East Coast and Pacific Coast	40¢ per half ounce
1848	Between post offices on the Pacific Coast	12½¢ per half ounce
July 1, 1851	Up to, and including, 3000 miles More than 3000 miles Local Drop Letters	3¢ per half ounce 6¢ per half ounce 1¢
April 1, 1855	Up to 3000 miles More than 3000 miles Local Drop Letters Compulsory prepayment of domestic postage	3¢ per half ounce 10¢ per half ounce 1¢
July 1, 1856	Compulsory prepayment of domestic postage by use of postage stamps	
July 1, 1863	Entire United States	3¢ per half ounce
October 1, 1883	Entire United States	2¢ per half ounce
July 1, 1885	Entire United States	2¢ per half ounce

(2) it may have been posted under a different rate, like circulars, periodicals, etc.; (3) the postal rating clerk may have made a miscalculation in the proper postage due; (4) the cover may have been tampered with or stamps may have fallen off or been erroneously replaced at some time; and (5) it may have been a deliberate or accidental overpayment or underpayment of postage due as figured by the mailing postal patron and/or by the receiving postal clerk.

U.S. FIRST DAY COVER DATES

My table of first day cover dates is meant to be representative, not comprehensive, of well-established first-day of sale and/or use of some popular U.S. stamps. With many early U.S. FDCs bringing four figure prices when auctioned off, it behooves the prudent philatelist to memorize or often refer to such tables so that a genuine but apparently unrecognized FDC won't be ignored as relatively "worthless."

Official Post Office Department records, if they can be found, offer good evidence for a given first-day of sale of a stamp issue. Covers aren't always reliable because a clerk may have made a mistake in dating or a cover may have been posted with a "pre-FDC" dated cancel due to illegal use of a new stamp before its official release date; or a cover postdated a day or two later may have been actually posted on the first day of issue but languished in a post office drop box over a holiday, etc.

Also, beware of forged dates for valuable FDCs, and of stamps affixed to a cover to make it appear to be a first day cancel; e.g., a common nondescript cover with a cheap stamp and several May 1, 1901 circular date handstamps on the envelope gets a Pan-American adhesive glued on it and becomes an instant Pan-American FDC!

UNITED STATES TERRITORIAL AND STATEHOOD DATES

Besides the original thirteen colonies whose statehood dates are effectively when each ratified the U.S. Constitution, the other states achieved statehood from time to time with or without Territorial status. A Territorial cover is especially desirable because it indicates early mail service in the soon-to-be new state. Pre-Territorial covers are equally important if not even rarer, due to the smaller population and more primitive postal system than would be developed under Territorial government. Both Pre-Territorial and Territorial covers are Pre-Statehood philately, and are worth serious study as postal forerunners of the future state.

Beware of forged and altered cancels to create instant "Territorial" covers. On the other hand, commitment to memory of the appropriate dates of Territorial status and Admission to the Union of the states in whose covers you specialize can repay itself well someday when you discover a Pre-Statehood item that has gone unrecognized.

I especially like to look at California covers or documents dated before September 9, 1850: California's Admission Day. Gold was discovered by James Marshall on January 24, 1848 and California had a Mexican, U.S. military, and civil government before statehood, thus never being a formal Territory. If somebody offers to sell you a California Territorial cover, they either don't know their history or are sloppy with political definitions.

SOME IMPORTANT U.S. FIRST DAY COVER DATES	
Stamp Issue	**First Day of Issue**
1847 5¢ & 10¢ General Issues	July 1, 1847, although none are known with that date
1851 1¢ and 3¢ Imperforates (depends on variety)	July 1, 1851
1869 Pictorials: 1¢, 2¢, and 3¢	March 27, 1869
1881 3¢ Blue green	July 16, 1881
1883 2¢ and 4¢	October 1, 1883
1887 2¢ Green	September 10, 1887
1890 American Bank Note Company definitives: 1¢, 2¢, 3¢, 6¢, 10¢, 15¢, 30¢ and 90¢	February 22, 1890
1893 Columbian Exposition Issues	January 2, 1893 (or January 1) except for 8¢ (earliest known use – March 3, 1893)
1898 Trans-Mississippi Exposition Issue	June 17, 1898 (all values)
1901 Pan-American Exposition Issue	May 1, 1901 (all values)
1904 Louisiana Purchase Exposition Issue	April 30, 1904 (all issues)
1907 Jamestown Exposition Issue	April 26, 1907, for 1¢ & 2¢. May 10, 1907 earliest known use for the 5¢.
1909 Alaska-Yukon-Pacific Exposition 2¢ stamp	June 1, 1909 for perforated, June 13, 1909 earliest known use for imperforate version.
1909 Hudson-Fulton Celebration Issue 2¢ stamp	September 25, 1909
1913 Panama-Pacific Exposition Issue	January 2, 1913 for 1¢, 5¢, and 10¢ values.
1919 3¢ Victory Issue	March 3, 1919
1920 Pilgrim Tercentenary Issue	December 21, 1920 (all values)
1885 Special Delivery 10¢ Issue	October 1, 1885
1911 Registration 10¢ Issue	December 1, 1911
1913 Parcel Post Issue	January 1, 1913 for parcel post use for most values, July 1, 1913 for first class use.
1918 U.S. Air Mails	May 13, 1918 for 24¢, July 11, 1918 for 16¢, December 10, 1918 for 6¢.
1923 U.S. Air Mails	August 15, 1923 for 8¢, August 17, 1923 for 16¢, August 21, 1923 for 24¢.
1930 Graf Zeppelins	April 19, 1930 (all values)
1933 50¢ "Baby Zeppelin"	October 2 through October 7, 1933, depending on city

UNITED STATES TERRITORIAL AND STATEHOOD DATES
(After the Original Thirteen States)

State Name	Made a Territory	Statehood
1. Alabama	August 15, 1817	December 14, 18919
2. Alaska	October 18, 1867	January 3, 1959
3. Arizona	February 24, 1863	February 14, 1912
4. Arkansas	July 5, 1819	June 15, 1836
5. California	never a territory	September 9, 1850
6. Colorado	February 28, 1861	August 1, 1876
7. Florida	March 30, 1822	March 3, 1845
8. Hawaii	August 12, 1898	August 21, 1959
9. Idaho	March 3, 1863	July 3, 1890
10. Illinois	March 2, 1809	December 3, 1818
11. Indiana	July 5, 1800	December 11, 1816
12. Iowa	July 4, 1838	December 28, 1846
13. Kansas	May 30, 1854	January 29, 1861
14. Kentucky	never a territory	June 1, 1792
15. Louisiana	July 4, 1805	April 30, 1812
16. Maine	never a territory	March 16, 1820
17. Michigan	July 1, 1805	January 26, 1837
18. Minnesota	March 3, 1849	May 11, 1858
19. Mississippi	May 7, 1798	December 10, 1817
20. Missouri	December 7, 1812	August 10, 1821
21. Montana	May 26, 1864	November 8, 1889
22. Nebraska	May 30, 1854	March 1, 1867

UNITED STATES TERRITORIAL AND STATEHOOD DATES (cont.) (After the Original Thirteen States)		
State Name	**Made a Territory**	**Statehood**
23. Nevada	March 2, 1861	October 31, 1864
24. New Mexico	December 13, 1850	January 6, 1912
25. North Dakota	March 2, 1861	November 2, 1889
26. Ohio	July 13, 1787 (part of the Northwest Territory)	March 1, 1803
27. Oklahoma	May 2, 1890	November 16, 1907
28. Oregon	August 14, 1848	February 14, 1859
29. South Dakota	March 2, 1861	November 2, 1889
30. Tennessee	(had been Southwest Territory)	June 1, 1796
31. Texas	never a territory	December 29, 1845
32. Utah	September 9, 1850	January 4, 1896
33. Vermont	never a territory	March 4, 1791
34. Washington	March 2, 1853	November 11, 1889
35. West Virginia	never a territory	June 20, 1863
36. Wisconsin	July 4, 1836	May 29, 1848
37. Wyoming	July 29, 1868	July 10, 1890

IMPORTANT MAIL SERVICE INNOVATIONS IN THE UNITED STATES	
Date Effective	**Service Introduced**
February 1, 1842	*First adhesive stamp* in U.S.: Alexander M. Greig's City Despatch Post of New York City.
July 1, 1845	Letter rates *based on weight* instead of number of sheets. distance zones reduced from five to two (less than, and more than, 300 miles).
July 1845	First U.S. *Postmaster Provisionals* under Robert H. Morris, New York City.
July 1, 1847	First *General Issue* U.S. adhesives, the 1847 5¢ Franklin and 10¢ Washington.
September 30, 1852	*Unsealed circular* uniform postage rate: 1¢ for 3 ounces anywhere in the United States.
July 1, 1853	First U.S. stamped *embossed envelopes*.
April 1, 1855	*Prepayment* of domestic U.S. postage made compulsory.
July 1, 1855	First U.S. *Registry System*, the fee being 5¢ plus the postage rate.
July 1, 1856	Compulsory prepayment of domestic postage by use of *stamps*.
1857	First *perforated* U.S. stamps.
April 1860-October 1861	The Western *Pony Express*.
1862	First U.S. *revenue stamps* (ignoring items such as Colonial embossed revenue stamped paper)
July 1, 1863	*Uniform letter postage* of 3¢ per half ounce for any domestic distance. Free letter carrier *city delivery* service in forty-nine of the larger northern cities.
1864	*Domestic money orders* from the Post Office Department; first maximum limit was $30.
August 28, 1864	First *Railway Post Office* (on the Chicago & North Western Railroad between Chicago and Clinton, IA)
1867	First U.S. *international money orders*.
May 1873	First U.S. *postal cards*.

IMPORTANT MAIL SERVICE INNOVATIONS IN THE UNITED STATES (cont.)	
Date Effective	**Service Introduced**
1874	*Universal Postal Union* founded (first known as the General Postal Union, named changed to UPU in 1878).
July 1, 1879	First U.S. *postage due stamps*.
October 1, 1885	*Special Delivery Service* started.
1894	*Bureau of Engraving and Printing* assumes production of U.S. stamps.
October 1, 1896	*Rural Free Delivery* begun as an experiment in West Virginia.

Chapter 3

Rare U.S. and Foreign Stamps

The first half of this chapter is devoted to rare and famous U.S. stamps; the second half to foreign rarities. Rarity isn't automatically equivalent to famous or expensive. Some U.S. and foreign locals are known by only a few copies but are relatively cheap to buy compared to the 1930 U.S. Zeppelins, for example. Some minor varieties ("fly-speck philately"), such as modern color shifts or misperforations or tiny plate flaws, may be essentially unique — only one known copy or block — yet command merely a moderate market price because of lack of demand.

There is no shortage of the 1847 U.S. 5¢ and 10¢ first definitives. Every good U.S. auction company offers frequent selections of them. It is just that the romance and collector popularity of our first stamps pushes their selling price through the roof, while truly scarce items like some U.S. Proofs (only hundreds or a couple of thousand made) or elusive Private Die Proprietary Stamps (Match & Medicine) go begging at a much lower retail value. I've decided to be traditional and discuss the *rare with expensive* items, in other words: items most philatelists would enjoy owning, but which few can afford.

U.S. POSTMASTER PROVISIONALS

Before the introduction and acceptance of regular U.S. government postage stamps, beginning in 1847, local American postmasters issued their own "provisional" stamps in certain cities. All are rare today, and some are unique, only one copy known, such as the 1846 5¢ Boscawen, New Hampshire uncancelled on cover, and produced by Worcester Webster, Postmaster of Boscawen; or the 1846 5¢ Lockport, New York (Hezekiah W. Scovell, Postmaster) which has one "sound" copy known, on cover. Surely the Boscawen and Lockport Postmasters may have sold more than a single provisional, but because none have turned up, they each fetch stiff five figure prices when sold.

The Alexandria, Virginia provisionals of Daniel Bryan (1846) are all cut-to-shape to form a "circular" stamp — a prime example of how a "damaged" stamp can still be valuable (remember the 1¢

British Guiana has its corners missing).

For sheer timeless beauty I happen to like the 1845 Baltimore, Maryland "James M. Buchanan" and the 1845-46 St. Louis "Bears" (John M. Wimer, Postmaster) *on cover*. The Buchanan provisional is simplicity itself, the entire design being the Postmaster's signature and "5 Cents." And the St. Louis Bears are so well-known that they attract attention and spirited bidding as they come up at auction. Sure, a fairly nice Buchanan or St. Louis cover might set your stamp budget back $5000 for one of the cheaper varieties(!), but you'll hold in your hand postal history of a kind that is recognized and desired around the world.

For a more limited budget, why not collect the New York City provisionals of Robert H. Morris (1845)? For $300 to $500 you can buy a decent example on or off cover. Or for several hundred to around a thousand dollars you can have the varieties of 1846 Providence, Rhode Island provisionals (Welcome B. Sayles, Postmaster). Be careful of reprints and forgeries of any U.S. postmasters' provisionals; get a certificate if you don't trust your own judgment.

ENCASED POSTAGE STAMPS

The patented invention of a young entrepreneur, John Gault of Boston, *encased postage stamps* capture the imagination as only a Civil War-inspired creation can. Dangerous fraud has been perpetrated on gullible collectors by unscrupulous individuals who (1) replace cracked or scratched mica (pristine, flawless mica is rare and commands a premium value); (2) substitute a low denomination stamp in the case with a higher denomination (30¢ and 90¢ values sell for thousands of dollars each); or (3) clean the whole case so it looks more or less uncirculated.

According to Bowers and Hodder, the average encased postage stamp of the U.S. Civil War period grades about VF. Stamp color may be faded, and mica may be "crazed," (hair line saturated), to some extent. The case itself may be scratched, bent, or badly discolored, all of which drop the value in proportion to the conspicuousness of the flaw. Grading is often hard to finalize about a given encased postage stamp because the grade is really a composite of the grades of the mica, case, and stamp.

Retail and auction prices lately for undamaged encased postage stamps run from $100 to $300 for the cheaper varieties in "fine" condition to $2000 and up for the scarce business names and/or high denomination encased stamps. They aren't unobtainable, but their rarity is shown by the fact that many stamp dealers

$1 Trans-Mississippi Exposition commemorative (Western Cattle in Storm) issued June 17, 1898. Immaculately clean, lightly cancelled copy. No faults in or out of fluid. Notice the centering and perforation conditions. This stamp approaches superb quality; for the discriminating philatelist. The author paid $750 for it in 1989.

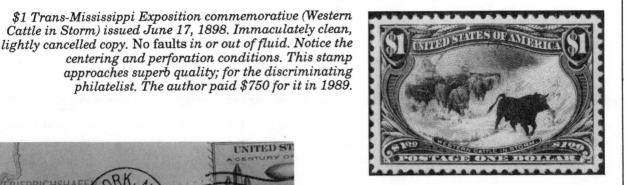

50¢ Graf Zeppelin cover showing the first-day-of-issue cancel of New York City, October 2, 1933. Notice how postmark ties the stamp to the cover. This stamp has different first-day dates, depending on the city where cancelled: October 4 for Akron, OH; October 7 for Chicago; October 6 for Miami; and October 5 for Washington, DC. Memorize first-day dates for stamps in your specialty.

Three copies of the 1¢ Franklin ultramarine American Bank Note Company issue of 1887 on 2¢ Washington green on white embossed envelope, cancelled Santa Monica, CA November 15, 1889 to London. Backstamped received in London, England 2 December, 1889 — about two weeks in transit, not much slower than some air mail letters would take today! Interesting docking, including at cover's top: "Posted 3 days before I was run down by a London bus and crippled temporarily." Stamp at left not tied, but undoubtedly belongs because it has similar shade and centering as the other two copies, and the seapost rate from America to England in 1889 was 5¢.

have no encased postage stamps in stock. You can collect encased postage stamps by business name, by denomination, by country area of use; you can seek one of each major variety (a "type" collection) or try to exhaust the possibilities for a single prolific company (like Ayer's Pills or Drake's Plantation Bitters).

Unless you fancy yourself an expert in this field, any expensive U.S. encased postage stamp absolutely must come with a recent expertizing certificate, either from the Philatelic Foundation (preferably) or the American Philatelic Society. And be careful of faked certificates or of an encased postage stamp that was altered after the certificate was issued (replaced stamp or repaired mica).

THE 1847 ISSUES

Whatever criticism you care to make about them, the fact remains that an exhibit of frame after frame of choice copies of the U.S. *1847 5¢ Franklin* and *10¢ Washington* is nothing less than awe-inspiring! Expense and philatelic romance are combined in the classic understated designs of our first two General Issue adhesives. For choice copies with wide margins and no flaws, the 5¢ brown value currently retails at $3000 to $5000 mint, $500 to $1000 used. The 10¢ Washington (in basic black, what else?) goes for around $10,000 or more with full gum, $1000 to $2000 cancelled.

But condition is all important for these imperforates; and stamps with surface scuffs, tiny thins, "sealed" tears, bleached-out pen cancels, heavy distracting "killer" cancels, or faked gum will sell at a steep discount from their undamaged cousins — *provided* that the seller/buyer is smart enough to detect these flaws. I recommend that you insist on floating in watermark fluid *any* 1847 appearing to be undamaged, and examine it with both strong incandescent front *and* back lighting.

The 1847's are especially nice in pairs, blocks, and on clean *unfolded* covers (with no distracting creases across the cover's face, not a reference to "folded covers" as an envelope-less term), but you had better have a deep wallet if you plan to specialize in such material.

19TH CENTURY HIGH VALUES

U.S. *19th century high values*, either mint or cancelled, on or off cover, are exquisite stamps. The 90¢ Washington blues of 1860 and 1861; the 90¢ 1869 Lincoln; the 90¢ Perry of the 1870s and 1880s; the dollar value Columbians and Trans-Mississippians; and the $1, $2, and $5 1894-95 definitives are the cream of the

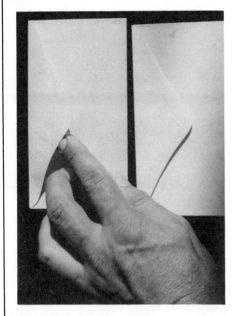

The reverse sides of the Civil War patriotics shown at right. Undamaged flaps with original gum, cracked and yellowed. No hinge marks as commonly found on even unused Civil War patriotics. Such covers in pristine condition are available for those who seek. Beware of post-war envelope reprints, which Raymond H. Weill warned me about when I asked him why he didn't have any unused Civil War patriotics for sale.

"Autographed" Civil War patriotics in immaculate condition. "George W. Adams, River Point, R.I., August 5, 1862" and "Rufus McIntire, Parsonfields, Me., Oct. 1st, 1863, Born Dec. 19th - 1784" pen inscriptions. Something different for the routine patriotics collection.

3¢ violet Victory Issue on a first-day cover, cancelled Washington, DC, March 3, 1919. Beware of forged or altered cancels to make early covers appear to be first-days. Also of stamps added to a cover that "happens" to be postmarked when the added stamps were issued. Memorize the first-day dates of stamps in your specialty.

1841 Great Britain 2-pence blue in strip of three, and 1-penny red brown in block of ten, cancelled and without damage. Photo doesn't show it well, but the 2-pence stamp on the left end of the strip (position SD) has its design clear of the margin all the way around. Usually found with defects like folds between stamps or scissors cuts, surface scrapes, tiny hinge thins. Buy them undamaged.

4¢ rose Washington adhesive of 1861 on a Wells, Fargo cover piece, tied by blue "COLLECT" box. The 19th century express company covers are always enhanced when they have stamps attached. For quality items, collect them with undamaged full-margined stamps, as in this example.

Wells, Fargo shipping tag for $160 (80 gold, 80 sil) dated December 4, 1877 (in pencil on front, in ink on the reverse). Collateral such as this may be frowned upon by exhibition judges, but it makes for an interesting collection to round out an album of Wells, Fargo covers.

high face value stamps that were sold in 19th century U.S. post offices. A specialized collection of any of these in any form: mint and used singles, shades, multiples including plate blocks, printing varieties including the 1875 Reissues and imperf. pairs — all would be a worthwhile exhibit or investment, and the envy of those who see them!

U.S. 19TH CENTURY WAR COVERS

War covers have perennial appeal, especially less often-seen ones such as battlefield mail of the War of 1812 or the Mexican-American War of the 1840s or the Indian Wars of the last third of the 19th century (perhaps a soldier's letter from the 7th Cavalry?). The Spanish-American War of the late 1890s provides many good patriotic covers.

The Civil War of 1861-65 generated a virtual paper avalanche of war mail, the best from a philatelic monetary standpoint being prisoner-of-war mail, Confederate patriotics, blocks and strips of Confederate adhesives on cover, "per flag of truce" and blockade-run covers, and mixed franking (Union and Southern postage) and wallpaper covers. A soldier's prolonged campaign, as shown by a long correspondence, can sometimes be as useful as a battlefield diary in reconstructing what he saw and did in the war.

MINING COVERS

Mining covers evoke visions of tired but determined prospectors and mules, mountain streams and desolate canyons, Indian raids and claim jumpers, with small pouches of gold dust and silver ore strung along their pistol belts as they swagger into a boom-town post office to hand the clerk a letter bound for missed relatives back home. California, Nevada, and Arizona mining covers of the 19th century are forever wonderful and magical with their hand-scrawled contents within, and their postage rates and addresses denoted on the envelope fronts.

At $700 to $1000, the average nice California Gold Rush illustrated, cacheted miner's cover is worth buying and studying if you can afford it. Such items are quite rare in XF condition, and will hardly be cheaper in time to come. The *Letters of Gold* cover exhibit which made the show circuit recently displayed the best in California miners' covers.

PONY EXPRESS

In the early 1970s you could buy, at auction, some of the most excellent Pony Express covers of the celebrated Western routes for around $1000. Gone are those prices; currently the nicer quality Pony Express covers with no damages run $4000 to $5000 and up. On or off cover, the Wells, Fargo Pony Express locals are always breathtaking and worthy of admiration by all who view them. Off cover Pony Express singles are remarkably cheap: $50 to $200, but beware of dangerous forgeries (get certificates when in doubt).

EARLY GREAT BRITAIN

Great Britain's line engraved 1840-56 issues with extra large margins for the imperforates, undamaged perforations for the others, are always good stamps to collect. Sizeable multiples in blocks or strips, mint or used, of the cheaper varieties make splendid displays. Early British covers are notoriously faulty with small-margined stamps, disfiguring creases and stains, or faded colors. An unblemished 1840s Great Britain cover with boardwalk margins on the affixed stamps, and *no* cover creases anywhere is magnificent. Key British rarities like the 1882 5-pound orange or 1884 1-pound brown-lilac (and later varieties) are imposing with no defects, especially mint with original gum.

CANADIAN PENCE ISSUES

The matchless Canadian rarities are the "Pence Issues" of 1851-59, issued under Province of Canada administration. Of special note is the 12-Pence Queen Victoria stamp of 1851: unused or used, it will cost around $50,000 for a specimen you can be proud of. You can tell who's serious about stamps when you notice a collector buying mint Canadian Pence Issues just to study the different paper varieties.

BRITISH GUIANA

It is through philatelic tradition as much as due to rarity that early *British Guiana* (1850-59) stamps are in such high demand. Also, you need these issues to have a "complete" British Commonwealth collection, so well-to-do collectors of the past century have been bidding the price up on the "Cotton Reels" and the "Ship" 1¢ and 4¢ cousins of the famed 1¢ 1856 Black on Magenta. You might well have to pay a quarter of a million dollars to get decent copies of the major varieties of these early British Guiana (not counting the 1¢ of 1856). *Provenance* helps here — I would be suspicious of any rare British Guiana stamp that suddenly appears without a pedigree of previous ownership. Was it stolen, is it fake, has it been repaired?

MAURITIUS

Some of the early *Mauritius* are actually affordable by collectors with moderate budgets: like the 6-Pence red of 1858 ($20-$30, mint or used), and defective copies (with "minor defects") of some of the other 1848-59 stamps. But the "Post Office" 1847 first issues command six-figure prices apiece, the stuff that the Weill brothers stock is built from! You see a lot of damaged early Mauritius offered at auction, but don't forget that what is cheap to buy is invariably cheap to sell, and may very well be a bad investment.

EUROPEAN RARITIES As far as Europe goes, some of the *French* Ceres heads of 1849-50 sell for upwards of $5000, and tête bêche pairs can push $50,000-$100,000. Nineteenth century *German States* covers are frequently emphasized in German and Swiss auction company catalogs, and the more unusual stamp combinations are delightful to read about, with the aid of a German dictionary if necessary. I happen to think the Nazi military locals (unlisted in Scott) are worth investing in; for instance, the Palm tree and Swastika "Afrika Korps" issues of Rommel's occupation forces are three-figure items off cover, rising to near $1000 for an immaculate tied-to-cover usage. This stamp, by the way, is almost always off center with sometimes rough perforations, so a mathematically centered copy should earn a premium.

The 1855 typographed *Swedish* stamps (even ignoring the real or faked 3 skilling banco orange) are all good properties, the better ones selling for several thousand dollars each; be wary of the cheap reprints, though. And the *Swiss Cantonals* of 1843-50 are undeniably sublime, with the better ones costing five figure prices; likewise, watch out for reprints, proofs passing as stamps, and outright counterfeits.

ASIAN RARITIES Nineteenth century Asian stamps are currently in great demand. Any scarce Japanese, Chinese, or specialty areas like Hong Kong have ready buyers. Unfortunately, dangerous counterfeits are common in early Japan, so buy them with certificates if you are not an expert.

50¢ Canadian Schooner "Bluenose" stamp of 1929. A selection of cancelled copies of better than average centering. Found in practically every auction of Canadian stamps, so be choosy when buying this issue: flawless copies, well-centered, with nice, clean full perforation teeth. Notice registry cancel on lower right pair.

At right, Mount Everest Expedition local label of 1924 in mint strip of three. Was printed in panes of 36 with selvage all around. Various shades of blue. Often off-center, but notice the nice margins on the center copy. When purchased on the Expedition post card, stamp should be tied by Expedition cancel. Try to find an undamaged card — most have corner bends or worse damage.

Kon-Tiki Expedition cover carried on board the raft Kon-Tiki from Peru to Polynesia in 1947. French Polynesian stamps cancelled Papeete, Ile Tahiti on August 26, 1947. Signed by Erik Hesselberg, Navigator on the raft Kon-Tiki. A quality expedition cover, purchased by the author at auction in the 1970s for about $150.

Chapter 4

Neglected Specialties

Often overlooked in the mad scramble for definitives, commemoratives, and air mails are the other aspects of philately that make for worthwhile specialty studies. Dead countries, unusual covers, back-of-the-book items, Proofs and Essays, catalog-unlisted material, postal stationery, and collateral are all touched on in this chapter. A collection should be as personal as its owner, and what better way to make your collections an emotional extension of yourself than to explore an area of philately that may be neglected by the majority of collectors and dealers.

DEAD COUNTRIES   *Dead countries* offer much to the determined philatelist who appreciates the opportunity to specialize in a country or political entity that: (1) is cheaper to collect than more popular realms like Japan or Switzerland; (2) may have less reference information published on it, and therefore is ripe for original research; (3) permits the publication in article or book form of the findings of the dead country specialist with less research necessary than, say, the United States or Great Britain definitive series; and (4) offers unknown challenges to the newcomer for the simple fact that so little may be known at present about the country.

There are exceptions, however: Confederate philately has been studied extensively in the 20th century; the former independent provinces of Canada have been more or less well investigated; and some German States like Bavaria have already had serious studies. New data is always being uncovered in even well-known dead entities, but some are more mysterious than others.

Little is known about certain U.S. Locals or about the war mail of obscure foreign war campaigns. When is the last time you saw an exhibit of non-philatelic Zululand covers with the 1888-96 adhesives? They exist, but are scarce and hard to track down in nice condition.

The Hawaiian Missionaries of 1851-52 cost thousands of dollars each, but an interesting showing of cancellation varieties of the cheaper Hawaiian issues would be a great specialty. Guam cancels on the 1899 Guam overprints would make a lovely exhibit, with or without covers. Quality Guam and Hawaiian material is expensive, but as dead countries their stamp output is fixed and frozen and offers a certain stability in philatelic study that "live" countries don't have. And because not every dealer has a huge stock of dead country stamps, the thrill of the chase for elusive varieties gives such a specialty an endless charm.

UNUSUAL COVERS

Covers from off the beaten path make wonderful collections. How about commercial (non-philatelically inspired) covers of the U.S. air mail issues of the 1930s? Have you ever seen a Baby Zeppelin (50¢ issue) on a business mailing cancelled in the 1930s?

Or a collection of illegal usages, like U.S. revenues and Christmas seals used as postage, demonitized use (like the Civil War "Old Stamps Not Recognized" covers), bisects, wrong stamp type (Special Delivery for Parcel Post service), foreign stamps on mail postmarked in another nation, cleaned and reused stamps on classic covers, and proofs or essays or postal stationery "stamps" pasted on covers.

A slightly unusual exhibit might be prepared of the 1938 U.S. Presidential definitives incorrectly calculated to pay rates of the period, i.e., over or under payment covers on non-philatelic origin. Or a collection of "mixed franking" covers of U.S. definitives of two adjacent series, e.g., a Presidential and a Liberty series stamp on the same cover, indicating the transition period.

A spectacular collection could be stamp errors used on covers without philatelic intent. Or a prize-winning exhibit of covers with the only on-cover known use of each stamp variety. Or legitimate scientific mail with complicated routing markings and handstamps — on covers from obscure expeditions, which didn't prepare philatelic souvenirs. Or, as I once owned, a collection of worldwide covers addressed to Adolf Hitler or some other infamous historical person.

BACK-OF-THE-BOOK ITEMS

How about an exhibit of forwarded covers? Or to be more traditional, postage dues on cover? The "back of the book," referring to the large section of items listed after the U.S. regulars, commemoratives, and air mails in the Scott *U.S. Specialized*, has untold opportunities for interesting collections. Telegraph stamps on and off telegrams, Officially Sealed mail, use of revenues on

2¢ Black Jack of 1863 tied on cover by segmented, quartered crossroads cork cancel. This stamp is not *doubly perforated, it is* misperforated *through the top of the design, then cut to shape, including the sharply cut perforation teeth on the left side of the stamp. Slight dry-inking around the numerals, which is common in Black Jack printings.*

2¢ Black Jack of 1863 tied on cover by geometric circle of wedges cork cancel. In the same color of brown iron-gall ink as used to address the envelope, this stamp is caricatured by outlining Jackson's facial features and the stamp's border itself. For the student of unusual Black Jack varieties. Cover addressed to: Jas. M. Chalmers, Esq., 56 John Street, New York.

2¢ Black Jack not tied by geometric rosette cork cancel on periodical advertising cover from Philadelphia's "The Age" on Chestnut Street. Cancel appears to have been removed from Jackson's face for reuse of the stamp. Evidence of dried glue traces around stamp's border supports reuse (or that this adhesive doesn't belong on the cover). Pencil notations on envelope's back: "1/76 Herman Herst, Jr $7.50" and "4-" indicate old purchase prices of cover.

Address side of Amundsen picture post card carried per SS "Fram" through Polar Ice. With "Polhavet" circular date stamp on Norwegian Posthorn Numeral adhesives of 1910: 1-ore, 2-ore, 5-ore, 15-ore, and 20-ore; and the 12-ore of 1917. Unlike most of these cards, this one is in remarkable condition, without the usual folds, surface scrapes, or bent corners. Facsimile of Amundsen's signature.

Uncanceled 10-ore brown Spidsbergen local stamp picturing an upright bear and armed man. Found on Norway covers circa 1900; most desirable on polar covers, usually ship covers. Beware of untied copies added to covers to raise their value.

Upper left corner of photo above, showing "Polhavet" circular date stamps tying the Norwegian Posthorn numerals on the card and Roald Amundsen's facsimile signature. Quality polar covers always have a market.

bank checks, Hunting Permit Stamps (Ducks) on original licenses, pre-World War II War Savings stamps, Private Die Match and Medicines, Playing Card Stamps on original card wrappings — these are a few excellent back-of-the-book specialties.

The Private Die Proprietary Stamps, for example, are notoriously awful in condition. Wouldn't you like to see an exhibit, of even the cheaper varieties, well-centered and completely undamaged, including full perforations? Or an auction of such items? I have a couple of nice medicine stamps, but it takes a lot of searching and patience to find them.

The Official Stamps of the 1870s can become a lifetime specialty study. The Weill brothers stock of them was handsome, but you can start from scratch and delve as deeply as you wish into the Officials: mint and used singles, shades and printing varieties, cancels, on cover use, and multiples and Proofs.

I know what I want to see at my next stamp show visit: a comprehensive exhibit of Sanitary Fairs, including mint and used, covers, all known Proofs, and rare varieties properly analyzed.

PROOFS AND ESSAYS

U.S. Proofs and Essays are well known via Clarence W. Brazer's *Essays for United States Adhesive Postage Stamps* (1941, reprinted 1977 by Quarterman). A large annotated album full of U.S. Proofs and Essays is still fascinating to behold in the sharpness and brightness of the design impressions. But why not specialize in the Proofs and Essays of a foreign country, maybe of a certain issue or stamp series? I'm partial to 19th century British Commonwealth Proofs and Essays, but any country will do if it interests you and you can afford it.

UNLISTED MATERIAL

There is a romantic appeal for catalog-unlisted material which yet has some claim to philatelic legitimacy, such as the Scott-unlisted New Zealand Antarctic Expedition issues of "VICTORIA LAND" and "King Edward VII Land" of the early 1900s. Catalog-unlisted stamps means that many dealers and collectors may be unfamiliar with such items, making them ideal for an impressive exhibit, and perhaps obtainable for lower cost than if the stamps were "mainstream," heavily promoted "investment" pieces.

It is common knowledge that foreign specialist catalogs list expensive varieties that may not be mentioned in another nation's catalogs; e.g., Stanley Gibbons has seemingly endless stamp varieties of British Commonwealth issues that Scott ignores. The same applies to such publishers as Michel (Germany), Yvert (France), and Facit (Scandinavian countries). For the philatelist seeking financial profit (or an approximation of it), the study of specialized catalogs can well repay the hours invested, because stamps that are unlisted in one reference may be listed in another.

POSTAL STATIONERY

Then there is postal stationery, not only of the United States, but also of the world. For a collector with limited funds, the postal cards and embossed envelopes in either mint or used condition can be an alternative to struggling with the country's expensive adhesives. True, some exhibit judges tend to "look down" on postal stationery when compared with classic stamps and covers, but to those who know, stationery is every bit as challenging and mentally rewarding as the collection of postage stamps.

I like cancelled postal stationery from dead countries, with clear, sharp circular date stamps, and pristine cover condition. Boer War (1899-1902) postal cards and embossed envelopes from both sides (British and Boers) are definitely philately by any informed definition!

COLLATERAL

Although exhibit judges may frown on collateral as too gimmicky and distracting from the stamps themselves, non-stamp items dress up and enhance the quality of a serious collection. Shards of burnt crash covers, Zeppelin pieces, official letters from postal authorities relating to your specialty, old postal scales, California Gold Rush artifacts to go along with your Wells, Fargo covers, leather mail bags from long ago carriers, broadsides, postal bulletins, old stamp society award medals and trophies, personal copies of philatelic literature "ex-the library of some famous philatelist" — these are things that round out and bring to life your conventional stamps and covers.

For example, I collect things made in the year 1849 as collateral to my California Gold Rush covers: coins, letters, California territorial documents including bills of sale and financial promissory notes, pistols (Colt Model 1849 Pocket Revolver, etc.), and newspapers. Also if they seem to be "of the period" circa 1849: old medicine bottles with original medicine in them(!), eyeglasses, pocket gold scales, leather and cloth money pouches (one of mine has the imprint of a Sacramento bank), gambling devices, and tableware. I've also got an old map of the mining districts in

California, and I'm currently looking for a nice old street map of San Francisco (circa 1849 of course) — the port of debarkation of ship travelers bound for the California gold fields, and maybe a local postmaster's diary from Stockton or other town.

Chapter 5

Fakes and Frauds

Besides outright counterfeiting of the entire stamp, various frauds are perpetrated on the gullible collector, including shaved proofs, altered cancels, regumming, reperforating, faked line pairs, faked plate numbers, faked inverts, covers with stamps added, etc. This chapter outlines some methods to detect such frauds.

REPERFORATING

A stamp which has been reperforated because of damaged perforations, an original straight edge, or "unbalanced" margins may have perforation holes and teeth that don't match in size with the perforations along the rest of the stamp. The holes may be too "clean" with teeth too "crisp" for the stamp's age, and a row of perforations on one side may be out of alignment with the parallel row on the opposite side.

Genuine holes may be round or oval, deep or shallow, cleanly cut or rough. Teeth that seem to be smoothly cut or sheared rather than torn from the neighboring stamps are suspect. A good method to help detect reperforating is to lay a genuine set of perforations over another stamp suspected of having been reperforated and see if the holes and teeth more or less "match."

Always use a metal or plastic perforation gauge that will not distort over time, as cardboard might due to gain or loss of moisture. The standard catalogs list the known perforations of all legitimate stamps issued by the world's countries, so an obvious check on potentially counterfeit perfs is to compare the stamp's measured perforation gauge with its official catalog gauge. Know, however, that stamps themselves may expand or shrink over time and may appear to have a slightly different gauge than you would expect.

FAKED GUM

The legendary ex-New York stamp dealer Herman Herst, Jr. says that stamp gum is the most valuable thing in the world, even more precious per ounce than uranium or diamonds. Since World

War II collectors and investors have been willing to pay a hefty premium for rare stamps with undamaged original gum, when compared with the same issues with slightly disturbed gum. Collectors in Europe or Israel will often pay three or four times the price for a stamp if it *appears* to have undisturbed, never-hinged original gum. Double the price of a U.S. Columbian if it goes from HH (heavily hinged) to NH (never hinged), even though nothing may be altered except the state of the gum on the stamp's back!

Or to put it another way, would you rather have two or three collections with some degree of hinging, or one collection never hinged? A thousand Columbians or 300, the identical stamps perhaps, except for their gum?

So stamps often have faked gum applied to resemble as closely as possible the gum on originals. Or the original gum may be carefully liquified and resmoothed by humidifying the stamp until the gum becomes soft enough to spread over the gum-roughened areas. Always compare the gum on a rare stamp with a known genuine example; this is what the expertizing services do if their examiners haven't memorized what genuine gum of that issue looks like. And gum varies not only with age (old gum tends to turn yellow, crack, and become more brittle), but with country: the gum on Spanish stamps from the year 1900 doesn't look exactly like the gum from U.S. stamps from that year.

Distinguishing traits of faked gum: it looks too good or too "new" for the stamp's age. It drips over onto the front of the stamp; genuine stamps have no gum smears on their fronts unless they have been accidentally moistened to the point of liquifying their gum. Regummed stamps often have the perforation teeth too stiff, lacking the natural softness and gentle raggedness of genuine teeth, evidence of recently added gum soaking into the edge of the stamp's paper fibers. And if the gum looks wavy or in abnormal thicknesses or covering thin areas of the stamp's paper (not watermarks), be suspicious.

Stamps that normally have gum skips, like U.S. issues from the 1930s, look strange with perfectly smooth white shiny gum. You don't expect to be handed a bundle of Penny Blacks or 1847 U.S. definitives with flawless, perfect NH original gum. I once sold a strip of three Black Jacks to a dealer who marvelled at the original NH gum, cracked and yellowed with age, although not "perfect" from a regummer's perspective.

A regummed stamp will sometimes feel stiff and lack the flexibility or "snap" of a genuine mint copy. Ultraviolet light examination will often reveal faked gum made of a different chemical composition than the original because it glows differently.

SEALED TEARS AND HOLES

It is common to repair a tear or fill a hole so that the stamp appears undamaged. Ultraviolet light will sometimes show the lines along which a tear has been glued. Holding a stamp up to a strong light source will often do the same. The time-honored method for detecting thins and tears is still to dip the suspected stamp into watermark fluid in a jet black tray, but don't confuse normal watermarks or heavy cancel lines for thins and tears. Heavy hinging is occasionally used to hide a thin, one reason many discriminating collectors refuse to buy an expensive stamp with heavy hinging attached.

ALTERED INKS

Stamp ink fades over the years, especially if exposed to light or air pollution, so you can't always tell by a stamp's shade if the ink is genuine. The common 3¢ Washington of 1861 comes in more shades than it was ever printed in, due to discoloration in almost 1½ centuries.

Ultraviolet light, watermark tests, dipping in plain tap water, and holding it up to the light are simple tests for studying a stamp's ink. Genuine ink should be uniformly smooth and without conspicuous light and dark areas on the stamp's design, unless it was originally applied more heavily, such as in the finely engraved lines in a President's head of the U.S. 1938 regular issue series.

Beware of chemically altered colors to create a faked shade, such as the rare *blue* color error of the 4¢ ultramarine Columbian. These are best sent for an expertizing certificate; there is sometimes a trace of a chemical bath or other incriminating evidence on a color-altered fake that can only be detected in an expertizing laboratory.

FAKED CANCELS

Good cancellation fakes are extremely difficult to detect. The finest forgers may have been clever enough to obtain some cancellation ink that matches the chemical composition of ink cancels of the stamp's time period. Long experience in handling and studying genuine cancels is the best insurance in determining what doesn't "look right."

If a stamp is on original envelope paper, the cancellation should extend evenly from the stamp's paper onto the envelope (or "piece"), tying on the stamp and helping to ensure it belongs on the cover. It is much easier to fake a cancel on piece than on a whole intact cover because the rest of the envelope isn't there to incriminate the forger.

The removal of a stamp's cancel to make it seem unused often leaves the stamp faded or too "bright" in color. Ultraviolet light may detect traces of the original cancel impression. Assume that a stamp that is costly in mint state compared with a used version may have had a machine, manuscript, or handstamped cancel removed, then may have been regummed to appear mint.

WRONG STAMPS ON COVER

A rather indistinct cancel is very inviting for a forger to employ to replace a cheap stamp with a more expensive one to raise the value of a cover. For example, a high value 19th century U.S. definitive might be substituted for a 3¢ issue to make what seems to be a high denomination on cover. An analysis of the postal markings, the cancels on the stamp compared with those that may be on the cover, and the addresses or other markings on the cover may show that such a high denomination couldn't be used on a local or lightweight envelope, but if all you have is the stamp cancelled on piece you can't be sure if the postage use is genuine.

Bisects on piece are always suspect because verifying data from the lost cover is lost also. Bisects *must* be tied to cover with a clear and obvious cancellation extending between the stamp's cut edge and the cover's paper. I don't trust a lot of bisects. I once bought a 2¢ Black Jack bisect on cover by a mail bid, and I returned it because it wasn't properly tied (and wasn't illustrated in the auction catalog).

FAKED COIL LINE PAIRS

The guide lines on flat plate U.S. coils were printed every twenty stamps to guide the perforating machines. A guide line between a coil pair is casually taken by many collectors to indicate a genuine coil, but nothing could be further from the truth, as the lines themselves are often faked.

First, check the perforation gauge of the coil to eliminate fraudulent gauges at the start, then compare the coil's straight edges with genuine examples: the flat edges shouldn't be too irregular in any respect, whether in microscopic examination of the paper fibers or in their "feel" compared with genuine coils. Or the faked coil edge may be too clean, showing a recent scissors cut.

The coil guide lines must be of the same ink color as the rest of the stamp. The lines have to be engraved, not penned in, so they should feel "raised" from the stamp's paper surface like all of the other engraved ink impressions on it. Guide lines were put on stamps *before* they were perforated, so guide line ink shouldn't drip over the edge of genuine coils. And guide lines should be very straight and sharply delineated without abnormally wide or narrow portions to the line's width. Genuine guide lines on engraved U.S. stamps shouldn't "bleed" into the paper — as faked lines might because of ink absorption by porous paper fibers.

SHAVED PROOFS Thick "cardboard" proofs are sometimes shaved down to resemble stamps. Their ink impressions may appear too bright and distinct, unlike the issued stamps. And a shaved proof may have paper areas of varying thickness or may lack the watermarks of the genuine stamps. And an altered proof will have to be perforated if its sister stamps were so issued, so faked perforations should be suspected. The paper of the proofs may not match the paper of the issued stamps, either in color or texture. And the shaved proof will have to be given a faked cancel or gummed if it is to masquerade as a stamp, and these added attractions may not look like genuine specimens.

EXPERTIZING ORGANIZATIONS The two largest stamp expertizing organizations in the United States are the APS Expertizing Service and the PF (Philatelic Foundation). Write to them for a list of their fees, enclosing a stamped self-addressed business (No. 10) envelope:

> American Philatelic Society Expertizing Service
> P.O. Box 8000
> State College, PA 16803
>
> Philatelic Foundation
> 21 East 40th Street
> New York, NY 10016

The APS takes stamps of the world, as well as United States issues. The PF specializes in U.S. philately and carries more "weight" in its pronouncements than the APS Service for verifying U.S. stamps. Expertizing certificates have been faked by substituting a different stamp and photograph, altering the information (catalog number, mention of defects, etc.), or faking the certificate outright. Check with the expertizing service if in doubt about the authenticity of a certificate.

A.P.S. expertizing certificate with the examiner's opinion that this Transvaal stamp is counterfeit. Besides counterfeit and reprinted Transvaal stamps from the Z.A.R. period (Boer occupation), beware also of counterfeit or altered expertizing certificates. Write the expertizing service when in doubt.

Chapter 6

Philatelic Exhibiting

Tips on preparing your collection for competitive exhibition, how to organize and write up the pages, safe and secure display, and attracting the attention of the judges are covered in this chapter. Many philatelists spend a lifetime and a lot of money in the accumulation of a wonderful collection, only to pass on without ever having exhibited it for the applause and instruction of the public. You don't exhibit merely for medals and trophies; you exhibit to make the most of a great collection – and to learn more about it yourself. At least you can't say that an exhibitor's collection isn't organized!

WHAT TO EXHIBIT

Step one in exhibiting is to decide what you intend to emphasize in the display. Is it a particular issue of stamps, like the "Bullseyes" of Brazil or the Hermes Heads of Greece? Is it a town's postal history from the stampless era through modern definitives on commercial mail? Is it a topic or generic category like expedition mail or medicine stamps? Is it a romantic theme like "Letters of Gold"? Is it a war like the Boer or Siberian campaigns?

After you choose a specialty, you must draw up a plan of attack: Can you reasonably acquire the necessary items in your lifetime? Can you afford them? Will the collection be "complete" insofar as your exhibit title delineates? Is it virtually impossible to get some elusive necessary item to make your exhibit an award-winner?

PREPARING THE EXHIBIT

A group of acid-free heavy stock album pages can be purchased from philatelic supplies dealers. Some exhibit rules prohibit plastic mounts on covers and stamps, so learn first if hinges only are required before you mount the collection. Obviously you wish to tell a story, so the exhibit must be prepared with a flow of logic. A display of the 3¢ issue of 1861 might start with essays and proofs, then large multiples of issued designs, then color shades, then printing varieties (double transfers, paper differences,

Envelope addressed to "Reichskanzler Adolf Hitler, Berlin" with the notation "personlich" (personal). 12-pfennigs carmine von Hindenberg adhesive tied by Pforzheim postmark of 18.9.33 (September 18, 1933), not quite eight months after Hitler was appointed Chancellor of the German Reich. The infamous Nazi dictator received an avalanche of mail from his own country and other nations, but he rarely answered any of it. The contents of this envelope are gone, and for all we know, the sender also, as Gestapo agents were sure to investigate any German citizen who was bold enough to criticize Hitler in writing, if indeed the contents of this cover were "incriminating."

A selection of Black Jacks with production varieties, on the plastic approval cards on which they are stored in the author's bank safe deposit box. Such approval cards with dimensions just under 3.25 by 5.75 inches fit all safe deposit boxes and allow easy sorting and instant access from the protection of your bank's vault.

Exhibition awards of ribbons, medals, and certificates are the least important reasons we exhibit our collections. The most important are to learn more about stamps and covers, and to teach others what we have discovered.

printed on both sides, imperf. pairs), then common and uncommon cancels off cover, then some spectacular covers showing domestic and trans-oceanic usages. And if you can't get all of these items, then you can't call your exhibit: "The U.S. 3¢ 1861 Issue in All Its Aspects."

Don't put too much or too little on a page, either in write-up or in stamps and covers. Too much detail can be distracting and confusing, too little can be embarrassing in its cheapness. Each page should be a lesson to the viewer, and should be able to stand alone in its own right. Prized pieces like rare multiples or unique covers may command a page unto themselves, but don't be pretentious and have a dozen pages with one tiny rare stamp per page.

Large covers present a problem in mounting for best visual effect: sometimes they have to be mounted diagonally merely to fit between the page's borders. And try to leave a comfortable margin between stamps and written text — and the 0page's borders. I like hand-lettered write-ups with careful printing on light gray quadrilled album pages, and always use jet black ink for timeless beauty. Typing or computerizing the write-up smacks of laziness and modern inattention to detail, although you see gold medal winners these days with typed text.

NEATNESS COUNTS

What's the use of doing a philatelic exhibit if you don't do it right? There's nothing wrong with taking a year or more, in your spare time, just to mount and write up a collection of stamps that has probably taken a lot longer to acquire.

It is irritating and insulting to the judges to give them sloppy writing, obvious erasures, previous hinge marks on pages, frayed page edges, smeared write-up ink, or poor alignment with the most important things of all, the stamps and covers! You may not win the Grand Award of the show, but every exhibit can be the epitome of neatness. If you can't make a neat exhibit, have someone else mount it and do the writing.

ETHICS IN EXHIBITING

Never lie in an exhibit. Don't try to pass off counterfeits as genuine examples, whether or not you think the judges have the expertise to recognize them. The Z.A.R. issues of Transvaal have been prolifically counterfeited, and it would take an astute exhibitor or judge to recognize some of the well-done fakes; that is still no excuse for misrepresenting them. And some countries may confiscate counterfeits if you exhibit them publicly, so find out about this in advance.

You don't have to make a stamp exhibit a footnoted term paper, but I see nothing bad about mentioning people who helped you with the work — within the text of the writeups; e.g.: "According to *Smith*, this variety is unknown imperforated." Also, it is good to have an introductory page and even a concluding page to a large exhibit to orient and guide the viewer.

Although the crowd may never know it, I believe it is a bit un-ethical to simply "buy" a ready made prize-winning exhibit and put your name on it and start raking in the medals for yourself. Some exhibit committees of stamp shows may allow anonymous exhibits to be entered, and the judges who have done their homework may think they are viewing the material of the previ-ous owner! If *your* name is proudly put on anything, it should be substantially your *own* work.

Ethics and morals also dictate that you *never* complain about the judges' decisions. If you do your best and don't win a top award, then swallow your pride and enter the exhibit in a different show. If winning is all that matters to you, enter your collection in a small show where it will outclass the cheap exhibits. What do you expect, that a judge will reverse his opinion because you are complaining? *It is* acceptable, however, to inquire courte-ously about the reasons why your exhibit was downgraded — *if* the judges feel like telling you their reasons!

SECURITY   Always insure an exhibit whenever possible, both in transit and while at the show. It may be difficult to get show insurance be-cause of the awesome liability of the show committee sponsor in the event of a major theft. Send a collection by mail or private express fully insured, or deliver it in person with an armed guard escort if the value warrants it. The better shows may have better security, but not necessarily. I haven't heard of an exhibitor hir-ing his own security guard to stand watch over his display at a show, but the show's guards inhibit the casual thief by their presence alone.

One big risk is overnight security for multiple day shows. Is the exhibit hall locked and impenetrable by amateur burglars? Does a security guard patrol occasionally? Can someone enter the ex-hibit area via another part of the hotel or exhibition building? Does the show committee properly "clear" the exhibit rooms of people at day's end?

For a collection worth a few hundred dollars it is pretentious to worry about security, but for a six-figure valued exhibit, I would have no qualms about discussing provisions for security with the exhibit chairman.

DISPLAYING DELICATE ITEMS

A fragile, irreplaceable stamp or cover needs special protection during exhibition. An inert plastic mount or pocket may be necessary to keep a rice paper stamp or ash-bordered crash cover intact. Special instructions must be left with the exhibit mounting crew to exert extra care in putting such album pages in the display cases. Shipping to and from the show may also have to be done with extreme diligence so your prized item isn't crushed or bent en route.

DETRIMENTS TO THE EXHIBIT

From the judges' viewpoint, there are many annoying aspects of a stamp exhibit: incompleteness, obvious errors in fact in the write-up, lack of neatness in writing or mounting, overlooking important observations of a stamp or cover, pretentiousness ("This is the rarest Postage Due in the world"), gaudiness (multi-colored write-up inks or distracting page border embellishments — unless you have an exhibit of circus topicals!), inclusion of undesignated counterfeits, boring write-ups, and lack of a "story" to the exhibit flow.

It is a sad fact of philatelic exhibiting that the most money has tended to win the best awards, i.e., an exhibit of U.S. classics will make many judges ignore the frames of 20th century plate blocks or cheap first-day covers. This attitude has been slightly changing lately, but if top prizes soothe your ego, you'll have a better chance of getting them on a limited collecting budget if you *thoroughly* prepare an in-depth display of philatelic material; e.g., a complete and exhaustive study of a 25¢ stamp (retail price) showing all conceivable combinations of cover usages, cancels, production forms (full sheets and panes, essays, proofs, artist's sketches), and errors/varieties.

THE AAPE

The American Association of Philatelic Exhibitors (AAPE) was founded in 1986, and has over 1000 members who support and seek more guidance in philatelic exhibiting. A quarterly journal and an "Exhibitor's Critique Service" are some of the membership benefits. For membership information and an application, write to: AAPE, Box 432, South Orange, NJ 07079

Chapter 7

United States Stamp Dealers

Here is a selection of stamp dealers worth visiting when you are in their towns. They are in business as of this writing and have reputations for serious stamp dealing. Personalities play a big role in philately, and if you can find one or more dealers with whom you are comfortable in stamp transactions, you are fortunate. Treasure such a relationship as much as your most expensive rarities in your stamp albums! Stamps can be replaced more easily than trust and good will. Virtually all advanced philatelists cultivate lifelong business "friendships" with certain dealers.

Call first before you visit, as many dealers travel or have odd business hours or prefer appointments for personal visits so they can have what you need when you arrive. Don't feel obligated to buy anything on the first visit, but remember that a dealer's time is valuable and a long visit that doesn't result in business is considered discourteous.

Of course, I have no financial interest in any of these companies, and none of them have requested to be included in this book, nor have they had any control about what I have said about them. There are many excellent stamp dealers I haven't mentioned, but these are some of the better known ones. Be sure to enclose a stamped self-addressed envelope when requesting information by mail.

George Alevizos
2800 28th Street, Suite 323
Santa Monica, CA 90405
(213) 450-2543

Public auctions, mail sales, and net price lists of unusual stamps, proofs, and postal history of the world, especially scarce Asian items. I have had several pleasant transactions selling my better Transvaal covers to Mr. Alevizos. Visits by appointment only in a modern office complex in Santa Monica. Metered parking is available nearby.

Americana Stamp & Coin Company (Jay Tell)
18385 Ventura Boulevard
Tarzana, CA 91356
(818) 705-1100

In business since 1958. Buys and sells stamps of the world, with good stocks of U.S. singles, proofs, and errors. Large full-service stamp and coin store. Has advertised every day in the *Los Angeles Times* since 1963. Believes stamps are undervalued and will rise in price when inflation returns. Huge stock of U.S. stamps, mint and used, in "self-service" displays. When I visited Mr. Tell, he had these items in a glass counter top: 1869 15¢ used invert (price: $13,900); 1901 4¢ Pan-American mint invert with specimen overprint, sound ($6950); and a complete set of bi-colored essays of the Trans-Mississippians ($3350). In his stock were a group of U.S. 1847 issues, and a number of plate blocks of the 50¢ "Baby" Zeppelin, and virtually everything in between. A lovely well-organized store with security locking doors, in an upscale Los Angeles shopping center.

Earl P.L. Apfelbaum, Inc.
2006 Walnut Street
Philadelphia, PA 19103
(215) 567-5200

Public auctions and mail bid sales of U.S. and foreign stamps.

Richard A. Champagne
P.O. Box 372
Newton, MA 02160
(617) 969-5719

Stocks U.S. classics. Does important stamp shows. An entertaining speaker at show seminars.

Christie's Stamp Department
502 Park Avenue
New York, NY 10022
(212) 546-1087

Beautiful auction catalogs of U.S and world rarities. Send $10 for a catalog by mail. Ask them for what's coming up in future auctions.

Colonial Stamp Company (George W. Holschauer)
5410 Wilshire Boulevard, Suite 202
Los Angeles, CA 90036
(213) 933-9435

The most prestigious exclusively British Commonwealth auctioneer in the United States. Auctions and want lists for British Empire stamps, 1840-1935.

Columbian Stamp Company
Box B
New Rochelle, NY 10804
(914) 725-2290

Private treaty of rare U.S. classics, including expensive 19th century multiples.

Downtown Stamp Company
44 Academy Street
Newark, NJ 07102
(201) 623-2389

Services want lists for U.S. and world issues, including cheaper and moderately priced items.

Richard C. Frajola
85 North Street
Danbury, CT 06810
(203) 790-4311

Exquisite auction catalogs of U.S. classic covers. Postal history at its researched best. These catalogs have received awards as philatelic literature.

Gold Medal Mail Sales
J & H Stolow
989 Avenue of the Americas
New York, NY 10018
(212) 594-1144

Mail auctions of U.S. and foreign stamps. Buying collections, estates, and rarities. In business since 1930.

Golden Philatelics (Jack and Myrna Golden)
P.O. Box 484
Cedarhurst, NY 11516
(516) 791-1804

Good stock of U.S revenues, including cheaper but elusive varieties, bought and sold. Present at important stamp shows.

Harmers of New York, Inc.
14 East 33rd Street
New York, NY 10016
(212) 532-3700

Third generation stamp dealers Keith and Alison Harmer run the New York office of this prestigious auction house. Harmers sold the first Louise Boyd Dale/Alfred F. Lichtenstein collection, the Alfred H. Caspary collection, and the Franklin Delano Roosevelt collection. Harmers conducts ten auctions per year in the traditional auction season from September through June (established before air conditioning and busy schedules made stamp collecting in the summer as popular as in the winter). About 1000 lots are in each sale, featuring all kinds of U.S. and foreign stamps, with emphasis toward better items. Harmers has operated in New York since 1940.

> Sam Houston Philatelics (Bob Dumaine)
> 13310 Westheimer, Suite 150
> Houston, TX 77077
> (713) 493-6386

Specialist in U.S. duck stamps. Modern store and office complex in a shopping center at the west end of Houston. Mr. Dumaine gave me a tour of his facilities when I visited, and spent 1½ hours answering my questions. Does thirty-five shows a year, as well as auctions and mail sales. Handles U.S. stamps, and has new issue service for state duck issues (700 customers). Retail walk-in trade and mail order.

> Ideal Stamp Company (Sam Malamud)
> 460 West 34th Street
> New York, NY 10001
> (212) 629-7979

Buying and selling stamps of the world, especially U.S., British, Israel, and United Nations.

> Robert G. Kaufmann Auction Galleries
> 540 Colfax Road
> Wayne Township, NJ 07470
> (201) 831-1772

Lovely color-illustrated auction catalogs of U.S. classic stamps and covers.

> Daniel F. Kelleher Company, Inc.
> 50 Congress Street, Suite 314
> Boston, MA 02109
> (617) 742-0883

U.S. and BNA stamps at auction. This company has conducted 600 public auctions; established in 1885.

Andrew Levitt
P.O. Box 342
Danbury, CT 06813
(203) 743-5291

Broker for rare U.S. classics.

Greg Manning Company
115 Main Road
Montville, NJ 07045
(201) 299-1800

Serious buyer of all nice stamp properties.

Jack E. Molesworth
88 Beacon Street
Boston, MA 02108
(617) 523-2522

Classic U.S. stamps and covers for sale, sent on approval with references. Mr. Molesworth is an old-fashioned dealer, believing in the integrity of private treaty business. Also stocks Confederate material in all price ranges.

New England Stamp Company
643 Fifth Avenue, South
Naples, FL 33940
(813) 262-6226

Specializes in covers of the world. Established in 1893, recently moved to Florida. Approvals sent per want list and submitted references. Store is in a beautiful avenue of shops.

Rasdale Stamp Company
36 South Street, Suite 1102
Chicago, IL 60603
(312) 263-7334

Frequent public and mail auctions of U.S. and world stamps. Extremely ethical; gives advances on large stamp consignments and prompt payment after auctions. The first stamp floor auction I regularly attended as a young collector.

Michael Rogers
340 Park Avenue, North
Winter Park, FL 32789
(407) 644-2290

Lovely stamp store, best collecting supplies I've seen in the South. Carries full line of U.S. and foreign stamps, with in-depth stock of Asian items. Comfortable store in an immaculate tree-lined "sidewalk" small shop district, four miles north of Orlando.

> John G. Ross
> 55 West Monroe, Suite 1070
> Chicago, IL 60603
> (312) 236-4088

The patriarch of Chicago stamp dealers, in business there for almost fifty years. U.S. and world stamps bought and sold. Mr. Ross was once the only dealer I could find who was willing to buy my small British Africa collection in plastic mounts without examining each stamp.

> Rupp Brothers Rare Stamps
> P.O. Drawer J, Lenox Hill Station
> New York, NY 10021
> (212) 772-9005

Nineteenth century U.S. classics by mail. Write for specific wants.

> Jacques C. Schiff, Jr., Inc.
> 195 Main Street
> Ridgefield Park, NJ 07660
> (201) 641-5566

Auctions of U.S. and foreign stamps and covers. Most famous dealer who specializes in U.S. errors. In business since 1947.

> Robert A. Siegel Auction Galleries
> 160 East 56th Street
> New York, NY 10022
> (212) 753-6421

America's premier auction house for classic U.S. stamps. Their auctions gross in excess of $10 million per year. In 1971 I rode a Greyhound bus from Chicago to New York just to attend one of their auctions, where I purchased a huge carton of old U.S covers, so heavy I could barely lift it. I think I paid about $160, and the present auction value would undoubtedly exceed $1000. I was impressed by the Siegel auctioneer's ethics in refusing to reopen a lot for bidding after it was officially declared "sold." I believe I was the only collector at this auction; the other bidders being dealers and auction agents. Auctioneers of the Josiah K. Lilly, Mortimer L. Neinken, and Saul Newbury stamp collections. In business since 1930.

> Superior Stamp & Coin Company
> 9478 West Olympic Boulevard

Beverly Hills, CA 90212
(213) 203-9855

Retail, wholesale, and auction of stamps of the world. Emphasis on rarities. The company that graciously allowed me to photograph their stock for my first stamp book, *Collecting Stamps for Pleasure & Profit* (Betterway, 1988). The serious stamp business in Los Angeles is done here. Superior has a reputation for somewhat ignoring the "small" collector, but that's mainly because this company caters to a more affluent clientele than many of the other stamp stores in Los Angeles. I've made small purchases ($25) at their store without feeling I was wasting their time, and they are happy to sell albums and kits for beginners. A luxury shop in every sense of the word, with free parking under the building for customers, and an armed guard on the premises. Publishes a frequent price list called *Money Talks*, an informative illustrated catalog of interesting stamps and coins for sale at fixed prices. I've made some great purchases out of this catalog, but things sell fast so phone your order in when you get the latest issue. Write for prices of their catalogs and lists.

Town & Country Stamps (John J. Rebello)
P.O. Box 13542
St. Louis, MO 63138
(314) 522-0289

Constantly buying large and small lots of stamps. Quick check by return mail. One of the few stamp companies that will buy just about anything in stamps, so long as it is worth at least a few dollars. Sells great mixtures and more expensive items also.

United States Stamp Company (Warren J. Sankey)
368 Bush Street
San Francisco, CA 94104
(415) 421-7398

Worldwide and U.S. mint and used, supplies, want lists serviced. On this same street since 1928. Mr. Sankey is the second generation, third owner of the company. Walk-in traffic is 60% of business. Mail order is 40%. Willing to help beginners get started in collecting.

Raymond H. Weill Company
407 Royal Street
New Orleans, LA 70130
(504) 581-7373

Raymond H. and Roger G. Weill are legendary brothers in the retail stamp trade. Their small shop in the antiques section of New

Orleans' French Quarter had these business hours posted: "10 AM-3 PM, Monday-Friday" and I arrived there without an appointment at 4 PM, but I noticed a gentleman through the front window, so I knocked on the door and he smiled and let me in. It was Raymond Weill, and he unselfishly gave me a full hour of his time for an interview.

Just he, his brother Roger, and a secretary work in this shop which has been at this location for over fifty years. I asked him what changes he has seen in stamp collecting during his years in the business, and he replied that (1) the public today has a greater appreciation of rare stamps, considering the top prices many rarities bring; and (2) fewer kids are entering the stamp hobby. He is disappointed that fewer children are interested in stamps compared with the youth of years ago, and believes that television takes a lot of attention of modern-day kids. But, Mr. Weill told me that he has never found a young stamp collector who is also a "juvenile delinquent."

Mr. Weill was friendly and talkative, just the opposite of what I expected from his conservative stamp ads and prestigious reputation. He said he believes that stamps are in a class with any rare work of art, and showed me his original Caspary auction catalog with his successful bids written in the margins. He has a good stock of U.S. and BNA issues (recently sold, but now being replaced), and for security the more expensive items are kept at a local bank vault. He supports the majority ASDA position that Scott's lowering of catalog prices was excessive in 1989 catalogs.

To my surprise, Mr. Weill said he is willing to deal with beginning collectors on a small budget if "they are willing" to deal with him. He said if his only business was the great rarities for which he is famous, he wouldn't do much business! He remarked that the 9% sales tax in New Orleans is the highest in the country except for New Orleans Airport: 10%.

He spoke of stamps with enthusiasm and affection, and showed me Scott's catalog photos of Postmaster Provisionals that he has owned, and for which he is willing to pay serious money to reacquire. He said that the U.S. Zeppelins are a good buy now for either collecting or investment, but that a truly superb mint set might be difficult to find. He does very little local business; most customers come from elsewhere.

I looked at the glass display counters in Mr. Weill's shop and noticed a selection of Confederate general issue adhesives on cover, some cheaper U.S. mint sets (like the 1943-44 Overrun Countries), and some classic U.S. covers in the $65 to $400 price range. I bought a few copies, including used multiples, of the 3¢ Victory issue of 1919, one of my favorite U.S. stamps for shades and on-cover usages.

He let me look at his stamp stock with a wonderful pair of custom-engraved stamp tongs, which he wouldn't sell to me because he only has a few pairs that he can't get anymore from his Paris supplier.

I decided to present Mr. Weill with a copy of my first stamp book, which had just been published, and he got excited and asked me to autograph it, carefully watching as I did so. I felt honored by this request, and pointed out that I am not as famous as he is, to which Mr. Weill said: "Well, I haven't written a book!"

> Irwin Weinberg Rarities
> United Penn Bank Building
> Wilkes-Barre, PA 18701
> (717) 825-2636

Specializes in buying and selling expensive U.S. rarities. Once served as the broker of the 1¢ British Guiana.

> Richard Wolffers, Inc.
> 133 Kearny Street
> San Francisco, CA 94108
> (415) 781-5127

Public auctions of U.S. and foreign. After the recent death of Mr. Wolffers, the company was reorganized and continues to do business with similar stamps and catalog format. A good auction to obtain nice U.S. material and seldom-seen items. Their catalogs are descriptive, well-illustrated, and pleasant to read. I bought my handsome Black Jack strip of three from them in the 1970s.

> Al Zimmerman
> 843 Van Nest Avenue
> The Bronx, NY 10462
> (212) 822-7333

Auctions of 19th and 20th century U.S. covers, including rare flights and scarce early first days. I met Mr. Zimmerman once, at a Siegel auction in New York City, and he later purchased a small group of stampless covers from me. He likes to auction things that haven't been on the market for a long time.

PHILATELIC LITERATURE

And for philatelic literature, try these dealers:

> Leonard H. Hartmann
> P.O. Box 36006
> Louisville, KY 40233
> (502) 451-0317

A "Philatelic Bibliophile"; a source for virtually all important stamp books, in or out of print. Publishes a detailed price list, and services standing want lists.

> Empire Group, Inc.
> P.O. Box 2529
> West Lawn, PA 19609
> (215) 678-5000

Publishes a yearly philatelic literature price list, my latest copy listing over 1500 titles. Many hard-to-find out of print books.

> David G. Phillips Company, Inc.
> P.O. Box 611388
> North Miami, FL 33161
> (305) 895-0470

Deals in U.S. covers and philatelic literature. Sells the basic important references for the U.S. stamp specialist.

Chapter 8

Foreign Stamp Dealers

These are some of the more prestigious foreign stamp dealers who stand ready to do business with intermediate or advanced philatelists. If you can't get current postage stamps of their countries, a courteous gesture when requesting a mail reply is to enclose a U.S. dollar bill or its equivalent in the appropriate foreign currency, which you may already have or can buy at a local money exchanger or coin shop.

>Argyll Etkin, Ltd.
>48 Conduit Street, New Bond Street
>London W1R 9FB England
>Telephone 01-437-7800

Postal history specialist dealer in British Empire stamps, covers, proofs, and stationery.

>John Bull Stamps, Ltd.
>G.P.O. Box 10009
>Hong Kong
>Telephone 5-8905767

Public auctions with emphasis on China and Hong Kong stamps.

>Corinphila
>Bellerivestrasse 34
>P.O. Box 1
>CH-8034 Zurich, Switzerland
>Telephone 00411/383 10 60

Specializes in auctions of Swiss and other Western Europe.

>Christie's Robson Lowe
>8 King Street, St. James
>London SW1Y 6QT England
>Telephone 01-839 4034

Auctions of fine British Commonwealth. Combining the long-established reputations of Christie's in the antique/art trade with Robson Lowe in the stamp business. I bought a handsome Transvaal mourning cover from their David Crocker sale in 1980.

Eastern Auctions, Ltd.
P.O. Box 450
Bathurst, New Brunswick E2A 3Z4 Canada
Telephone (506) 546-6363

Frequent mail auctions with a great variety of Canadian and Newfoundland specialty items.

Stanley Gibbons Auctions
399 Strand
London WC2R OLX England
Telephone 01-836 8444

Auctions of excellent British Commonwealth. Walk-in shop sells stamps of the world in all price ranges and comprehensive collecting supplies. Bills itself as the "World's Largest Stamp Shop" and was recently remodeled. Who hasn't heard of Stanley Gibbons?

Harmers of London
91 New Bond Street
London W1A 4EH England
Telephone 01-629 0218

Auctions with quality British Commonwealth as well as foreign stamps.

Johnson Philatelics
P.O. Box 13450
Humewood, Port Elizabeth 6013, South Africa
Telephone 041-533159

Rare stamps, covers, and proofs of British Africa. Want lists invited.

Heinrich Köhler
Bahnhofstr. 63
D-6200 Wiesbaden, West Germany
Telephone 01149-6121-39381

Oldest stamp auctioneer in Germany, founded 1913. Auctions of German, other European stamps, and air mails.

R. Maresch & Sons
330 Bay Street, Suite 703
Toronto, Ontario M5H 2S9, Canada
Telephone (416) 363-7777

Established 1924 and bills itself as "Canada's Premier Auction House." BNA auctions and worldwide retail.

J.R. Mowbray, Ltd.
P.O. Box 63
Otaki Railway, New Zealand
Telephone 069-48270

Advertises itself as "New Zealand's Leading Auction House," established 1965. A good source of elusive Australia/New Zealand area stamps.

Phillips
101 New Bond Street
London W1Y OAS England
Telephone 01-629 6602

Auctions of worldwide stamps and covers, with emphasis, of course, on Great Britain.

Rudolf Steltzer
Rudolfstr. 13-17
D-6000 Frankfurt (Main) 11, West Germany
Telephone 069-234131

Auctions of better Germany and Western Europe.

Warwick & Warwick, Ltd.
Chalon House, 2 New Street
Warwick CV34 4RX England
Telephone 0926-499031

Auctions of British and worldwide stamps in moderate price ranges. Established 1958.

Chapter 9

National Stamp Societies

Membership in a philatelic society is a mark of distinction and pride for the serious philatelist. Some collectors point with honor to their twenty- or thirty-year-old membership, which they still maintain in good standing. Books borrowed or bought, auction catalogs and price lists subscribed to, and the weekly philatelic press faithfully read will leave the collector with something yet missing in his or her progress as a student of postage stamps. It is society membership, the club journals read, and the conversations or mail correspondence done with fellow members that complete the maturation of a stamp collector.

It is assumed that membership in the well-known and long-flourishing organizations, like the APS, American Air Mail Society, AFDCS, American Revenue Association, ATA, Bureau Issues Association, UPSS, and U.S. Philatelic Classics Society, will sooner or later be acquired by those whose collecting interests coincide with what is offered by these famous societies as outlined in my first book, *Collecting Stamps for Pleasure & Profit*. But here are a couple of dozen more groups — organizations that offer much in knowledge and inspiration to people who take the time and effort to uncover their wares; send a self-addressed stamped business-sized (No. 10) envelope for a membership application form, and the information on current dues.

American Association of Philatelic Exhibitors
Box 432
South Orange, NJ 07079

Official journal is *The Philatelic Exhibitor*, issued quarterly. A recent issue had John Hotchner providing comments from twenty-five gold medal winners on how to win a gold medal in stamp exhibiting.

American Society of Polar Philatelists
Box 945
Skokie, IL 60077

Ice Cap News bimonthly journal dealing with worldwide polar stamps, cancels, and covers. A recent issue dealt with Tristan da Cunha covers and Chinese Antarctic research expedition mail.

> Booklet Collectors Club
> 1016 E. El Camino Real, No. 107
> Sunnyvale, CA 94087

The Interleaf quarterly journal covers booklet panes of the world, a rather popular specialty lately.

> British North American Philatelic Society
> P.O. Box 1070
> Hay River, NT X0E 0R0 Canada

BNA Topics is an excellent bimonthly journal; a recent issue discussed Canadian telegraph covers, WWI and WWII postcards, and Newfoundland's 1932 stamps. This society sponsors books and sales circuits.

> Christmas Seal and Charity Stamp Society
> P.O. Box 41096
> Sacramento, CA 95841

Seal News bimonthly journal. Handbooks, slide programs, and sales book circuits.

> Essay-Proof Society
> 225 S. Fischer Avenue
> Jefferson, WI 53549

The Essay-Proof Journal quarterly publication for the serious essay-proof specialist.

> France and Colonies Philatelic Society
> Box 364
> Garwood, NJ 07027

France & Colonies Philatelist quarterly journal. Expertizing, handbooks, and slide programs available.

> Germany Philatelic Society
> P.O. Box 915678
> Longwood, FL 32791

The German Postal Specialist monthly journal. Expertizing, awards, slide programs, and handbooks published.

> Hawaiian Philatelic Society
> P.O. Box 10115
> Honolulu, HI 96816

Po'Oleka O Hawaii quarterly journal. Expertizing and society handbooks.

> International Society for Japanese Philately
> P.O. Box 1283
> Haddonfield, NJ 08033

Japanese Philately bimonthly journal. Expertizing and sales circuits available to members.

> Machine Cancel Society
> 9635 E. Randal Street
> Columbus, OH 47203

Machine Cancel Forum quarterly; recent articles dealt with Iowa Flag cancels and machine cancels in WWI.

> Medical Subjects Unit
> Box 6228
> Bridgewater, NJ 08807

A popular topical organization for medical professionals. Their bimonthly journal is quaintly named *Scalpel & Tongs*, a recent issue of which provided a checklist for Red Cross stamps of the world, and medically-related bulk mail imprints.

> Mexico-Elmhurst Philatelic Society International
> 2350 Bunker Hill Way
> Costa Mesa, CA 92626

Mexican philately at its organized best. *Mexicana* journal published quarterly; recent articles included foreign mail (1875-85), Mexican postmarks (1874-1900), and first Hidalgo issues. Handbooks, expertizing, awards, and sales circuits.

> Perfins Club
> R.R. No. 1, Box 5645
> Dryden, ME 04224

The Perfins Bulletin appears ten times a year and deals with worldwide perforated initial stamps. Sales circuits, club auctions, and awards.

> Postal History Society
> 8207 Daren Court
> Pikesville, MD 21208

Postal History Journal is the society's official publication, issued three times a year. Recent articles in it include Thurn & Taxis accountancy marks, and Hungary's inflationary postal rates.

Post Mark Collectors Club
2341 Grandview Road
Crest Hill, IL 60435

PMCC Bulletin issued monthly to members; a recent issue discussed Oklahoma cancels and USPS special cancels.

Royal Philatelic Society of Canada
P.O. Box 5320, Station "F"
Ottawa, Ontario K2C 3J1 Canada

The Canadian Philatelist bimonthly journal has been published since 1950; it is in English with occasional use of French. Over 100 chapters of this society across Canada. Traces its roots back over a century, with the present RPSC name adopted in the 1920s. Has a sales department for use by its members, conducts philatelic seminars, offers stamp insurance for Canadian members. Like the APS, bank and character references are needed by new applicants. Serious Canadian collectors are devoted to this organization.

Royal Philatelic Society, London
41 Devonshire Place
London W1N 1PE England

The London Philatelist, the society's bimonthly journal, has been published since 1892. The oldest stamp society in the world, established 1869, and called its present name since 1906. Maintains a handsome library and museum on the premises, and its Expert Committee has been in continuous operation for almost seventy years. Journal articles heavily slanted toward British Commonwealth issues. Publishes books of lasting value, like *British Guiana* by W.A. Townsend. Promotes British exhibitions, and annually awards three prestigious medals: the 26th Earl of Crawford, the Mr. T.K. Tapling, and the Mr. J.A. Tilleard Medals. Not to be confused with the RPS of Canada (see above).

Society of Israel Philatelists
3813 Bushnell Road
Cleveland, OH 44118

The Israel Philatelist published bimonthly; recent articles in it touched on Israeli postage dues, a 1942 postal card to the Theresienstadt camp in Bohemia, and the Haifa and Jaffa postmarks of the Palestine Mandate.

Space Topics Study Unit
Box 241
Maspeth, NY 11378

Astrophile is the society's official journal, issued bimonthly, and covering space topicals and space cancels.

> Trans-Mississippi Philatelic Society
> Box 164
> Council Bluffs, IA 51502

The Trans-Mississippian journal is published five times a year. Founded in 1934, the society has local chapters, an annual convention, and gives membership awards. Most members are from the Midwest, but most states are represented in this society.

> U.S. 1869 Pictorial Research Associates
> 3348 Clubhouse Road
> Virginia Beach, VA 23452

The 1869 Times appears quarterly. Handbooks, awards, and slide programs are society benefits. For the serious student of the U.S. 1869 issues, many of whom are also members of the U.S. Philatelic Classics Society.

> United States Possessions Philatelic Society
> 8100 Willow Stream Drive
> Sandy, UT 84092

Quarterly journal called *Possessions* deals with U.S. possessions philately. Recent articles include Christmas seals of the Philippines, Spanish postal cards in Puerto Rico (1878-98), and U.S. military government in Korea.

> Universal Ship Cancellation Society
> 35 Montague Circle
> East Hartford, CT 06118

U.S.C.S. Log monthly journal; recent articles include a discussion of harbor cutters of WWI era, and German Naval covers of 1919-45. Specializes more in the 20th century than, say, the Classics Society, which emphasizes 19th century ship covers.

> Zeppelin Collectors Club
> P.O. Box A3843
> Chicago, IL 60690

The Zeppelin Collector quarterly journal. Club auctions.

Chapter 10

Museums and Libraries

Here are some of the more important museums and libraries, which are renowned for their philatelic collections, in literature and/or in stamps and covers themselves. Call or write before visiting so you can be sure they will be open and ready to serve you when you arrive.

For examination of stamps and covers and rare documents it is necessary to apply in advance for an appointment; usually a month is sufficient, but short notice may suffice. All public libraries have sections on stamp collecting, and many museums have a few specimens of postal history as an accessory to their other exhibits, but the following institutions have the best.

NATIONAL PHILATELIC COLLECTION

National Philatelic Collection
National Museum of American History
Smithsonian Institution
Constitution Avenue (between 12th & 14th Streets)
Washington, DC 20560
(202) 357-1796

STRENGTHS OF THE NATIONAL COLLECTION

America's national stamp collection is housed in the Smithsonian Institution. Many important philatelists over the years have contributed to this collection, and the materials are available for study by serious researchers. Highlights include proofs and essays of U.S. stamps, study collections of 20th century revenues, U.S. precancels, and Zeppelin and rocket mail. The National Philatelic collection is strong in Afghanistan, Australia, Belgium, Chile, Colombia, Ecuador, Napoleonic France, Germany, Indian Feudatory States, Indonesia, Roman States, Japan, Latvia, Israel, Liberia, Nepal, Panama, Paraguay, Peru, and the Philippines. Notable topical collections are Rotary stamps of the world, music on stamps, and Red Cross issues.

Researchers wishing to study the stamps and covers in the National Philatelic Collection must schedule visits at least two weeks in advance, with specific requests so the staff will have the

Stampless folded cover wrapper (contents clipped away) from early California statehood. Red circular "SAN JOSE Cal. AUG 28" postmark with penned "5" indicating five cents postage collect. Mailed to the Secretary of State, "Cty of Valaho, U. Cal" (City of Vallejo, Upper California). Founded in 1850 by M. J. Vallejo, the city that bears his name was the California state capital in 1851 and 1852. These are facts that might be overlooked by a casual browser with a dealer's box of stampless covers.

Medical advertising cover, U.S. Medicine Co., New York City. Cancelled March 3, 1900 with flag cancel (the stripes of which are the origin of our wavy line cancels), addressed to Pleasant Green, Phillips Co (County), Kan (Kansas). This cover, of course, traveled in the mail system by railroad train because the airplane was invented in 1903. A popular collecting specialty, medical covers should be clean and undamaged to bring top dollar.

California Bicycle Mail local of 1894 with retouched die (San Francisco spelling error corrected), signed by Arthur C. Banta (Fresno agent for Victor Bicycles), who established this local post service; and by O.J. Treat, the stamp's printer. And a copy of the defaced genuine die, which is unknown in used condition (not to be confused with defaced counterfeit die).

appropriate material ready. Research may be done by appointment only and at no charge, on weekdays between 10:00 a.m. and 12:00 noon, and between 1:30 p.m. and 4:00 p.m. Security is strict to prevent theft: a staff member will be with the researcher at all times, and camera surveillance is done in the reference area.

RESEARCH RULES

Bags, books, coats, briefcases, etc. must be checked in the office prior to working with materials. Only soft lead pencils and paper for note-taking are allowed in the work areas. Because stamps and covers are delicate, nothing may be laid on top of them, and all materials must be handled with extreme care. Photocopy service at 25¢ per page may be done at the discretion of the staff, and with their assistance. Useful equipment like microscopes, watermark detectors, ultraviolet lamps, and stamp tongs will be *provided* by the staff for the researcher's use. Smoking, eating, and drinking are forbidden near the collections.

But besides original philatelic items, the National Philatelic Collection has a large library of rare and unusual volumes related to philately, including state postal histories, U.S. Post Office Department files, patents relating to the mails, and original documents in stamp design and production. The library has on microfilm many stamp periodicals, auction catalogs, and philatelic exhibition programs. A photograph and slide archive has over 10,000 illustrations which can be reproduced. Three-dimensional postal artifacts are also available for study, including postal vehicles(!), maps, mailboxes, canceling machines, and postmen's uniforms. The staff may require that you use gloves when handling such objects.

HALL OF POSTAL HISTORY

Of course, the general public sees only a tiny part of the National Philatelic Collection via the *Hall of Postal History and Philately* located on the third floor of the museum. Stamps, covers, and postal artifacts are selected by the staff for constantly changing exhibits. The exhibit area is open every day except Christmas, 10:00 a.m. to 5:30 p.m. with free admission. Because the National Philatelic Collection has over 16 million specimens, it can only display a small fraction of them at any given time.

I especially enjoy looking at the great rarities on exhibit, and the reference collections in sliding panels along the walls of the Hall of Postal History. When I was last there, they had a visitor-activated lighting system for certain rare stamps, so that the stamp ink wouldn't fade from constant light exposure, a persistent problem with any paper materials on exhibit in museums.

No trip to Washington, DC is complete without a stroll through the Smithsonian's stamp exhibits.

CARDINAL SPELLMAN MUSEUM

Cardinal Spellman Philatelic Museum
235 Wellesley Street
Weston, MA 02193
(617) 894-6735

At a stamp show in Anaheim, CA, I once heard Herman Herst, Jr. tell a philatelic joke with the punch line having to do with a collector who vowed he'd never get married, and then revealed himself as Cardinal Spellman! In this museum are housed the personal collections of the Cardinal, President Eisenhower, and Jascha Heifetz, as well as much more donated material to the tune of 30,000 volumes. Three exhibit galleries are open to the public, with other materials available for research by appointment with the museum staff.

The Cardinal Spellman Philatelic Museum is open to visitors Tuesday through Thursday, 10:00 a.m. to 4:00 p.m., and Sunday 1:00 p.m. to 5:00 p.m. Admission is free, but donations are requested. Museum memberships are available for interested supporters.

Every spring, this museum sponsors a two-day "Philatelic Literature Fair" in which recent stamp publications are exhibited to the interested public. I received a handwritten note from the museum for my 1990 book donations; the corresponding secretary wrote: "We were so pleased to receive the four copies of your new book *Stamp Collecting*, and are looking forward to entering them in the Fair . . ."

In the thirty years of the existence of the Cardinal Spellman Philatelic Museum, it has established a well-organized collection and library, improved its exhibits, and sponsored traveling exhibits. It also publishes and distributes philatelic literature, which it regularly advertises in Section 166 of *Linn's* classified ads.

THE COLLECTORS CLUB

The Collectors Club
22 East 35th Street
New York, NY 10016
(212) 683-0559

Established in 1896 by a group of New York City philatelists, the Collectors Club is a prestigious membership organization that promotes the best in philately. Its library of over 140,000 items is the largest specialized philatelic library in the world, located on the second floor of the Club-owned building. This organization produces outstanding publications of lasting value, including a bimonthly journal, *The Collectors Club Philatelist*. During the year, the Club produces twenty philatelic programs, and bestows awards like the Alfred F. Lichtenstein Memorial Award for "distinguished philatelic service."

The Club maintains a lounge with comfortable chairs and sofas, tables, and desks for study by members. The Club's Publicity Committee supplies the philatelic and general press with stamp information, and the Club gives stamps and philatelic supplies to schools and hospitals for use in recreational therapy. Annual dues are $100 for a person residing or working within a fifty mile radius of Columbus Circle, New York City; and $35 for those residing and employed beyond fifty miles. Membership applications require two references and two proposers who are members already.

The Collectors Club library is open to the public on Monday, Wednesday, and Friday from 10:00 a.m. to 4:00 p.m., but on the first and third Wednesdays of the month hours are from 1:00 p.m. to 8:00 p.m. Appointments must be made to use Club stamp material for research. The library is closed legal holidays and from June 15 through September 15.

APS LIBRARY

American Philatelic Research Library
100 Oakwood Avenue
State College, PA

mailing address:

APRL
Box 8338
State College, PA 16803

The APS Research Library is the largest general philatelic library in the United States open to the public. The library staff handles more than 17,000 requests per year for loans, copies, and searches. Materials include handbooks, catalogs, and philatelic periodicals. APS members may borrow library materials by mail by paying a moderate fee for shipping and handling.

The Library publishes a quarterly journal, the *Philatelic Literature Review*, which is sent to members of the Library. The Library is open Monday through Friday, 8:00 a.m. to 4:30 p.m.; Saturday 8:00 a.m. to 12:00 noon; and is closed on Saturday from November 1 to March 1. Photocopy service is available at 20¢ per page.

It is amazing how many APS members have never visited or otherwise used the services of their society's Library!

WESTERN POSTAL HISTORY MUSEUM

Western Postal History Museum
920 North First Avenue
Tucson, AZ 85719
(602) 623-6652

mailing address:

WPHM
P.O. Box 40725
Tucson, AZ 85717

As if you needed another excuse to visit the clean and pleasant southern Arizona desert city of Tucson, the Western Postal History Museum, founded in 1960, houses postmarks and covers from western states, with emphasis on Arizona, as well as specialized collections of Mexico, Canada, and the United Nations.

The quarterly publication, *The Heliograph*, contains informative articles and a calendar of museum events. The museum produces philatelic publications, and conducts stamp courses in local public schools. The museum library is open to the public on weekdays from 8:30 a.m. to 4:30 p.m. (closed on national holidays).

Permanent museum exhibits are located two blocks away at the Arizona Heritage Center, 949 E. Second Street, Tucson. These exhibits are free to the public Monday through Saturday 10:00 a.m. to 4:00 p.m., Sunday 12:00 to 4:00 p.m. Museum members receive a discount on museum publications, such as the 272-page *Arizona Statehood Postmark Catalog* by Bechtel, with 3721 illustrated postmarks of the 1912-82 period.

WESTERN PHILATELIC LIBRARY

Western Philatelic Library
Sunnyvale Public Library
665 West Olive Avenue
Sunnyvale, CA 94086
(408) 730-7300

Established in 1969 and merged in 1971 with the Philatelic Research Library, the friends of the South Bay Philatelic Library changed its name to the Friends of the Western Philatelic Library. It is now the proud philatelic section of the Public Library at Sunnyvale, CA (just north of San Jose at the southern tip of San Francisco Bay). It houses more than 5000 bound volumes, over 800 of which circulate to library card holders. Occasional displays of philatelic material can be seen in the library's lobby.

The Library is open to the public Monday through Thursday 10:00 a.m. to 9:00 p.m.; Friday and Saturday 10:00 a.m. to 6:00 p.m.; Sunday 1:00 p.m. to 5:00 p.m. Closed on holidays.

WELLS, FARGO MUSEUM

Wells, Fargo Bank History Museum
420 Montgomery Street
San Francisco, CA 94104
(415) 396-2619

Ernest A. Wiltsee left in trust his collection of over 1300 covers with the stipulation that they be used for public display. This is now the Wiltsee Memorial Collection of Western Stamps, Franks and Postmarks. It includes 235 different express companies and such fascinating items as Pony Express stamps and early California "ghost" town cancels. Open to the public Monday through Friday, 9:00 a.m. to 5:00 p.m. Closed on bank holidays; free admission.

CANADIAN POSTAL ARCHIVES

Canadian Postal Archives
365 Laureen Avenue West
Ottawa, Ontario K1A 0N3 Canada
(613) 995-5138 (Information number)

Part of the National Archives of Canada, the Canadian Postal Archives is available to researchers by appointment. The Archives houses a library of 10,000 philatelic volumes, as well as a large collection of Canadian stamps. Hours of use are Tuesday through Saturday 10:00 a.m. to 5:00 p.m. Free admission.

BRITISH LIBRARY

The British Library, Philatelic Collections
Great Russell Street
London WC1B 3DG England
Telephone 071-323 7635/6

Over six million items are in the spectacular British Library

Philatelic Collections, including the Thomas K. Tapling Collection of 19th century stamps of the world. Tapling was the most important British philatelist in his time, and when he died in 1891 he bequeathed his 200 volume collection to the British Museum where it has remained to this day. The Tapling Collection is essentially complete in basic varieties from 1840 to 1890, and is strong in British Commonwealth rarities like the "Post Office" Mauritius and Western Australia 1854 4d. frame inverted error.

Stamps not on display in the King's Library gallery may be seen by appointment. About 80,000 items on 6000 album sheets (including 2400 from the Tapling Collection) may be viewed on exhibit display Monday through Saturday, 10:00 a.m. to 5:00 p.m.; and Sunday from 2:30 p.m. to 6:00 p.m. Closed holidays. Free admission.

The British Library holds over 20,000 volumes of philatelic literature, including about 4500 volumes in the Crawford Library. Bequeathed in 1913 by the 26th Earl of Crawford, the Crawford Library may be the most complete collection of philatelic literature in the world dealing with the 1861-1913 time period. This literature may be examined with a Reader's Pass in the Reading Room on Monday, Friday, and Saturday 9:00 a.m. to 5:00 p.m.; and Tuesday, Wednesday, and Thursday 9:00 a.m. to 9:00 p.m. Photocopying is not permitted for material in the Crawford Library nor for any philatelic item proper.

OTHER FOREIGN MUSEUMS

Many foreign capitals have postal museums, and a visiting philatelist should endeavor to find them. For example: Vienna, Brussels, Copenhagen, Helsinki, Paris, Berlin and Bonn, The Hague, Oslo, Lima, Lisbon, Bern. These museums generally have specialized exhibits of philately of their own nations' stamps.

Chapter 11

Shipping Stamp Collections

When selling, trading, donating, or sending stamps for expertizing or loan collateral, it is often necessary to pack and ship a collection with due regard for safety and expediency. This chapter gives tips from my personal experiences of a lifetime of sending hundreds of stamp shipments to dealers, other collectors, auction houses, loan companies, and even my publisher.

SELECTING A CARRIER

The choice of a commercial transport company isn't something to be taken frivolously. You entrust your treasured stamps to the fate and fortunes of strangers when you ship collections across the country or to other nations. Let's look at UPS, Federal Express, private courier, and the USPS.

UNITED PARCEL SERVICE

United Parcel Service (UPS) has those brown delivery trucks zipping around all major U.S. cities, and the company has earned a reputation for delivering packages faster, cheaper (but only a little these days), and with less incidence of damage than the Postal Service. As a school teacher, my first choice of transport for any school supplies has always been UPS. I find they rarely damage parcels, and their rates are competitive if not lower than any other transport company for comparable service for a given size and weight package.

UPS gives automatic insurance indemnity for up to $100 for anything shipped by them. If the customer declares the value at time of shipment, UPS will further extend the insurance coverage at the rate of 25¢ per $100 over the initial $100 free insurance. So, for an extra dollar, you can send a $500 valued package via UPS, fully insured against loss or damage in transit. This is definitely a good choice for albums or large cartons of covers with a total replacement value in this price range.

Several liabilities with UPS are that they don't deliver *everywhere* as the Postal Service does, and you have to be near a UPS dispatching office to take advantage of their services (there are more post offices around), although many of the "pack and mail" services offer shipment. UPS also has Next Day Air and 2nd Day Air service available at higher cost. I would feel very safe sending a small stamp collection of moderate value via UPS.

FEDERAL EXPRESS   Federal Express Corporation, with its sharp-looking purple, orange, and white logos, has revolutionized air express shipments in the few years it has been in business. The brainchild of CEO Fred Smith, Federal Express is a Memphis, TN based private company with New York Stock Exchange listing, and "drop off" and "delivery" centers in virtually all major U.S. cities. For example, there are sixty-seven fully staffed Federal Express drop off locations in the Los Angeles area where parcels may be taken for entering the delivery system. I use the one on Wilshire Boulevard in Santa Monica, which is open until 6:00 p.m. on weekdays, 5:00 p.m. on Saturdays.

Federal Express also delivers customs-cleared parcels to many communities in Canada, Europe, the Far East, the Middle East, Africa, Australasia, Central and South America, the Caribbean, and Mexico. Federal Express provides airport-to-airport freight services for air cargo in conjunction with air freight agents and forwarders.

The most convenient thing about Federal Express service is a virtually guaranteed next day delivery in the continental U.S., with "Priority Overnight Service" for the next business morning, and "Standard Overnight Service" for delivery by next business afternoon (and a little cheaper than morning delivery). A bargain as far as safety and reliability in transmission are concerned is Federal Express "Economy Service" for second business day delivery; I use the Economy Service for shipping copies of my stamp books to philatelic exhibitions and book fairs.

An "Airbill" with a package tracking number receipt is given to Federal Express customers at the time of shipment, and this company is unique among commercial carriers in providing on-demand information on the location of any shipment at any given time. Their computer tracking systems even monitor Federal Express international shipments so they can tell you where your shipment is at any second when you inquire!

Federal Express also has account privileges for frequent users, with preprinted airbills, discounted rates, and courier pickups scheduled in advance. With proper identification, Federal Express drop off centers take payment by check, money order, or credit card (MasterCard, VISA, American Express, Discover, or Diner's Club) as well as cash. They also may take heavier packages for both domestic and overseas destinations than the Postal Service.

Federal Express doesn't *insure* shipments, but they offer to replace or repair up to $100 of value at no extra charge, and up to $500 in value for $2.50 extra charge. Collectible stamps are prohibited, a definite drawback in using Federal Express for shipping stamp collections.

On the other hand, you can ship albums and accessories (over 150 pounds) by Federal Express, while the Postal Service limits you to seventy pounds for either first (priority) class or fourth (parcel post) class. As a practical matter, heavy stamp albums or common bundles of first-day covers can be shipped by Federal Express, but I would use registered mail for anything valued at over $500. Federal Express has a 24-hour toll-free information number: (800) 238-5355.

PRIVATE COURIER

A personal messenger or courier may be used to hand-carry an envelope of rare stamps or a volume of philatelic material by air plane, or for bulky collections, by armored car. For example, a dealer wishing to sell out his stock of worldwide sets in twenty metal filing cabinets may elect to transport his material by truck or armored car to the prospective purchaser. Or a philatelist who wishes to consign a great rarity to an auction firm across the country might fly it there himself, neatly and unsuspiciously tucked in his carry-on briefcase, or hire an agent to do the same. Private couriers are expensive, though, and usually charge by the hour, so it usually makes more sense to ship rarities by registered mail and have full insurance thrown in as part of the deal. Couriers may be used for shipments across town or a few blocks away.

U.S. POSTAL SERVICE

And so we come to the old standby, our U.S. Postal Service. Postal rates may be cheaper than UPS, and the Postal Service has the enviable selling point of delivering to any address in the world that can receive mail. Packages tend to receive the roughest handling in the mails, however, and I always pack well any stamps that I send by Postal Service.

The biggest advantage to sending stamps by registered mail is the high insurance coverage indemnities. The Postal Service will insure a parcel worth thousands of dollars, and registered fees for up to $1000 are only $5.25 plus the postage charge based on weight. When the Hope Diamond had to be transported to the Smithsonian Institution, it was sent by registered mail.

Registered mail is the safest way to send anything in the Postal Service: the contents may be fully insured against damage or loss, and security is maintained at every step of the way because each Postal employee must sign for the registered item when it changes hands. In all of the years I've been sending and receiving stamps by mail, I've never lost a registered parcel in either direction.

One caution: Don't put sealing tape over the flap of a registered envelope because the window clerk needs to handstamp the flap's edge with a circular inked stamping device to inhibit tampering with the envelope's contents. If you have a large parcel or need to tape it shut, try to use *first class insured* mail; the USPS provides insurance liability up to $500 for insured first class items. And send *nothing* by fourth class mail; it takes forever to get there and doesn't look very nice when it arrives; pay the extra money for first class mail.

I once shipped a large carton of covers by fourth class mail to a dealer in New York City who reported it damaged and partially "missing" on arrival. I had insured it at the main post office in Santa Monica, CA, and after the dealer and I filled out the appropriate claim forms, I was promptly paid by the Postal Service for the cost of the missing covers. You must inspect a stamp shipment immediately upon its arrival, either at your home or place of business, or post office box, and report at once any apparent damage or loss of contents in order to claim insurance payment.

PACKING SINGLE STAMPS

Securely *packing* philatelic material is the first step in sending it far away. Single stamps, strips, and small blocks should be carefully inserted into a plastic approval card (for sale at all stamp shops), then wrapped inside a protective envelope with *several* layers of cardboard of file folder thickness or greater *on each side* of the approval card, then placed inside a *heavy outer envelope* and securely sealed for transmission through the mails or other service (UPS, etc.). It should not be easy to bend the completed envelope when it is ready to go.

The outside of the envelope's front should
capital letters with waterproof ink with this information: (1) sender's name, address, *and* zip code; (2) recipient's name, ad

dress, and zip code; (3) carrying directions such as: FIRST CLASS, DO NOT BEND (I have red-inked handstamps with these words). Be sure to leave room on the envelope's face for postage stamps or meter stamp, and the insured or registry stamp or sticker.

You always run the risk when you use philatelically-inspired adhesive stamps on a valuable envelope that someone inside or outside the Postal Service may steal it because it looks like "stamp collector" material. Insurance or registration makes this problem somewhat irrelevant, but if I was nervous about a rare stamp being stolen from my mail, I would send it as unobtrusively as possible. Leave off any reference to a "stamp company" on the envelope, use meters or common definitives for postage, and make no mention of the contents on the outer envelope, except for insurance or registry sticker.

And if you are sending the envelope *insured* by USPS instead of registered, heavily tape the back flap shut with pressure-sensitive mailing tape to guard against it opening up during transmission. Large envelopes sent by first class mail (called "priority flats" in postal talk) should be clearly marked "FIRST CLASS" on *both sides* so they don't get stuck with third and fourth class slow-moving mail. Mail automatically goes by first class if it is not otherwise marked, but I like to be safe and make it obvious that I want and am paying for first class service.

PACKING ALBUMS   In packing albums, cover cartons, or other bulky philatelic items, the important thing to emphasize is the *strength* of the *outer box*. With Postal Service weight limits at seventy pounds, and Federal Express and other private carriers with weights even higher, it is entirely conceivable that your box of first-day covers may be placed underneath a box that weighs fifty or more pounds! Marking "FRAGILE" and "DO NOT STACK" all over the parcel doesn't guarantee that some busy clerk won't put heavy packages on top of yours anyway. You don't have to be able to stand on your box, but the box should be sturdy to weather the bouncing around during shipment that happens even with the most careful handling by conscientious crews.

A flimsy shirt or shoe box is no good for shipping a stamp album across the country. Two corrugated cardboard boxes, nearly the identical size and fitting one within the other, are a great start in packing bulky philatelic materials.

Enough internal "packing" padding must be inserted so that the album won't shift its weight during handling. Crushed cork or styrofoam, crumpled newspapers, and even clean towels make ideal packing padding. You should be able to turn the package over in any direction and not hear or feel the album "slide."

A cover letter and a detailed packing inventory sheet must be packed where they will be found and not torn, so I like to insert these documents (along with a business sized, No. 10, self-addressed stamped return envelope) into a manila file folder and then into a large envelope which I carefully paper clip or tape to the front cover of the album, or the top of the cover carton, etc. It is not a bad idea to print or use address stickers for your name and address — on the first page of *each* album or small box enclosed in the outer one — so that the recipient won't get your shipment mixed up with someone else's.

If you don't care about the stamps you are shipping, why should anyone else? Proper packaging with neat and strong materials shows that you are a careful person as well as an enthusiastic philatelist. Your package should stand out from all the rest when it arrives by "saying" "Open Me! I'm Important! I contain valuable stamps!"

Chapter 12

Finances

An ever-present thought in the mind of a serious collector is *finances*. While money is usually not the major reason we collect things (except for strict investments), the financial aspects of collecting expand and limit what we possess and what we can do. While it is quite possible to be a "pure" student of philately, like Walter Breen in our sister hobby of numismatics (he has probably forgotten more about coins than most affluent coin collectors will ever know!), the thrill of the chase, the joy of possession, and the convenience of handling and "experimenting with" our own stamps lead us inevitably to the details of finances. This chapter deals with record keeping, taxes, obtaining loans, stamp donations, and investment management.

KEEPING RECORDS *Record keeping* keeps your stamp finances orderly and immediately "inspectable." Inadequate records keep you forever wondering just what you own, whether or not you made a profit on the sale of that ten-year-old cover, and what is the present status of the "completeness" of your collection and, by implication, what your acquisition goals should be for the near and distant future.

A Sample Record Sheet The *Stamp Record* section, beginning on page 145, is of my design, although you can modify it to suit your particular needs. The categories seem logical, and provide useful reference information long after the transaction has been forgotten.

"Collection Item #" refers to the collector's personal rare stamp acquisition number, much like a museum file number. In the example given, this was the 408th stamp purchased. Since it can't be found in any major catalog, it is designated "Unlisted." The Item Description may be as long or as short as you wish. "Postal State" means a shorthand symbol like: ** (mint, NH), * (unused), ⊙ (cancelled), ⊠ (on cover), ⊞ (block), etc. The example on page 145 shows that we have an unused block of four, i.e., a never cancelled block without gum. Condition should always be the *owner's opinion*, to give some consistency to the records because grading standards vary from person to person; convert an auction description or dealer's opinion into *your own condition* statement for your record sheet.

Price Paid and Date Purchased are essential to know how much money you have been spending on your choice material. "Where Purchased" means the dealer's or collector's name and, if necessary, address. "Other Remarks" include comments on the item's scarcity, doubtful attributions, where it "fits" in your collecting goals, etc.

Besides this information, you might want to add three more columns for: Date Sold, Price Sold, and Where Sold in order to keep profit/loss data straight. In addition to a detailed record sheet, you can enter your collection's inventory into a computer and/or also keep a pocket checklist by catalog number of what you have, to take with you when you go shopping. Or you can have a small index card file box with pertinent stamp data on 3 x 5 or 4 x 6 cards. The point is: *Keep Records.* You shouldn't have to hunt for an hour to discover what you have or don't have in your collection.

APPRAISALS

If you ever have formal *appraisals* done, these should be kept in manila folders in a file cabinet, maybe with photocopies also in your bank safe deposit box. You can have individual rarities appraised and cross-indexed by "Collection Item #" to your *Stamp Record* sheets or to your computer inventory. Or you may have a whole album or carton of covers appraised and so noted in the *appraisal section* of your file cabinet.

Most dealers will be happy to appraise a valuable collection, for a fee of course (which may be waived if you later sell the collection to them). It is important to specify what kind of written appraisal you desire: catalog value, replacement value, wholesale value, retail value. Is the appraisal being done for *insurance* purposes? To estimate prices realized if the collection was *auctioned* off today? For evaluating the collection for *trading* purposes if you intend to trade the material for other material? For IRS donation deductions? Tell the dealer when you are negotiating for an appraisal just what type of appraisal you need. Fees may run from 1% to 5% of catalog value, depending on the size of the collection, its value, and the effort required by the dealer to evaluate the material. A rough estimate of appraisal fees must be obtained in advance, and any ethical dealer will do this.

PROFITS AND LOSSES *Profit and loss* records must be maintained to declare capital gains profits or investment losses for federal income tax purposes. The tax laws are constantly changing, and each taxpayer's financial situation is unique, so I can't offer specific advice for buying or selling stamps to maximize tax benefits, but here are some general observations.

You can offset profits with losses in a given tax fiscal year, and for long term capital gains/losses as well. For example, if you make a net profit of $400 on one stamp, and lose $300 on another stamp, then you can most likely declare a total profit of only $100 for capital gains purposes. If investment is an important part of your collecting goals, don't be afraid to sell items at a loss in order to reduce capital gains on other material, and in order to sink that money into something better. Why hold an expensive stamp that keeps dropping in market value if investment profits are important to you?

INVESTMENTS A diversified stamp portfolio is sensible and more fun to assemble as well. For the long term, say ten or twenty years, it might be nice to buy some classic 19th century U.S. and British colonies singles, some Civil War Union and Confederate patriotic covers in immaculate condition, a few air mail plate blocks of the scarcer issues, and some rare early 20th century first-day covers. Then chart the price movement of this portfolio as time goes on, based (1) on what similar material is bringing at auction or (2) periodic objective third-party appraisals.

Investing at all in stamps is a controversial topic, and some dealers and established philatelists advise against expecting any profits when you go to sell rare stamps. Others are a bit too optimistic in their display ads and public pronouncements. It is true that stamps don't fluctuate as much as stocks or coins in a month or a year, on the average. It is also a fact that quality stamps have tended to rise in value over time, *provided* that the buyer didn't overpay when he bought the material.

Basically, anything that is rare and in demand at auction is prime material for investment consideration. I like to look at the price track record to decide what stamps seem best for investment. While nobody can see the future, wouldn't you like to own these things twenty years from now, especially if bought at a fair price today?

SOME SUGGESTED "INVESTMENTS"

VF mint or lightly cancelled *undamaged* 19th century U.S.; well-centered mint early U.S. air mails; early Great Britain and her present and former colonies, minimum current retail price of $100 per stamp; Wells, Fargo and other early Western express company covers, California Gold Rush covers, and Pony Express mail; U.S. Columbian and Trans-Mississippian stamps — well-centered *undamaged*, mint or used; better Zeppelin stamps and covers of the world; U.S. encased postage stamps; major catalog-listed errors costing over $500 each; and expensive foreign classics with certificates.

PHILATELIC DONATIONS

There are many non-profit organizations that will take stamp donations for either (1) use directly as therapy for patients, etc. or (2) for sale to raise cash for the organization's budget. From time to time, there have been fraudulent "charities" set up to swindle stamp donations from unwary collectors, so investigate the legitimacy of an organization before you donate by asking local Better Business Bureaus and Chambers of Commerce if they have heard of the charity, by writing to the editors of the stamp weeklies with similar requests, and by asking the organization itself for a financial statement or formal document showing that they are classified as a non-profit agency able to solicit tax-deductible donations according to current IRS rulings.

Children's hospitals, churches, veteran's organizations, schools, and scouting groups have been welcome recipients of stamp donations for years. Some even have a specific "officer" designated to process and acknowledge donations from the public. And remember, the full current appraised market value of the stamps may be possible to deduct on your income tax forms, depending on current IRS rules. So if you bought some stamps long ago and they have greatly increased in value, it may be wiser financially to donate them outright rather than first selling them, paying a capital gains tax, and then donating the net balance to your favorite charity.

A word of caution: I would hesitate to send stamps through the mail to a "first-time" advertiser in the classified section of the stamp weeklies. It may be a fraudulent organization which never intends to use the stamps for charitable purposes. Also, many legitimate organizations welcome the donation of collecting supplies like albums, catalogs, tongs, glassine envelopes, and hinges, all of which have some value for tax deduction purposes.

Many non-profit philatelic organizations welcome stamp and cover donations: the APS, national and local societies that auction members' material, the Philatelic Foundation, and the Collectors Club of New York — all accept donations for their reference collections. Be sure to include a detailed "invoice" of donated items, and it is a good idea if an officer of the receiving organization can sign and verify a copy of the donation inventory for your tax records.

LOANS Banks and employee credit unions may be willing to make loans with stamps as collateral, but they will probably want an appraisal first, and even then may not give a small loan (say, less than $1000) because of bookkeeping overhead. The philatelic press from time to time runs ads of companies that make loans on stamp collection collateral, and these companies are a ready source of quick emergency cash for the collector. You can also receive a substantial loan (thousands of dollars) for collections that merit it. Just send your stamps by registered mail, well-packed (see Chapter 11), and within a few weeks at the latest you will likely receive a check by return mail — in an amount that the lender feels appropriate based on his estimate of the current market value of your material. You should ask for a loan amount a little less than current wholesale value for a speedily-approved loan. Interest rates vary, depending on which company and in which state the loan is obtained, but expect rather high rates for such personal loans, maybe 1½% to 3% per month (similar to or a little less than pawn shop loan charges).

One reliable company I have gotten loans from over the years is:

S.H. Engel & Company, Inc.
P.O. Box 4
New Rochelle, NY 10804
(914) 632-2401

They are registered in the state of New York to make such loans, and are diligent about notifying their customers when the loan repayment is coming due. The loan receipts of Engel & Co. state: "If this loan is not repaid in full within 6 mos. from date, the collateral will be subject to sale after due notice. At any time within 6 mos., this loan may be repaid with interest due. Upon payment of the interest due, a new ticket . . . will be issued." This means the loan can be renewed indefinitely at stated rates of interest.

Another company that makes loans on stamps, licensed by the Banking Department of the Commonwealth of Pennsylvania, is:

Edelman's
301 Old York Road
Jenkinton, PA 19056
(215) 572-6480

One more thing: a nominal amount, maybe 1% of the loan's principal, will likely be charged for (1) vault storage; (2) insurance while the stamps are in the loan company's possession; and (3) appraisal costs, whether done on company time by the company's loan officers or by an outside party.

Chapter 13

Photographing Your Collection

You can always hire a professional photographer, as I did for my first stamp book, and pay hundreds of dollars to have your choicest stamps photographed at the time and place you request. The professional will bring everything necessary to take flawless close-up pictures of stamps or covers in slides or prints, and even throw in the negatives as part of the deal.

Or you can save a bundle of money and get the experience and satisfaction of doing it yourself, as I did for my second book. Also, you have complete freedom when you do your own photography — to choose the time and location, to preserve privacy and anonymity (if desired), and to take hundreds of shots at basically the expense of the film and commercial processing. This chapter explains how to photograph a stamp collection in your own home.

EQUIPMENT NEEDED A 35mm through-the-lens reflex camera (like most 35's sold in camera shops), a set of extension tubes that fit the camera's body, the basic 50mm or 55mm lens that comes with the camera, and some film are the minimum requirements for *stamp photography equipment*. A tripod or copy stand to keep your camera steady would be the next item to buy, but this isn't strictly necessary (in spite of what "everybody" recommends), as I'll explain later. Then you probably want two small lamps with a light-directed shade (or floodlamps themselves), that use normal household incandescent bulbs (I like 100 watts per bulb minimum wattage). These lamps should be able to stand on a desk or table, or be attachable to the table's edges if you want a more permanent setup. Finally, if you want to go all out, a special microlens or bellows might give you the most satisfactory results, but these aren't essential for most stamp photographic purposes. A teleconverter is a good compromise between extension tubes and special closeup lenses.

THE EASIEST METHOD

I've never seen this method described in print, but this is how I've been photographing my collection for years, and I haven't heard any complaints from newspaper and magazine editors who use my photos, or from stamp club audiences where I've given slide show lectures. It takes a steady hand to get away with this method, but it is cheap and simple to perform.

All I do is hand-hold my Pentax ME Super camera with my Vivitar 2X Macro Focusing Teleconverter attached between the camera's body and the normal Pentax 1:1.7 50mm lens (with no filter or other obstruction in front of it). Then I stand on top of a small wooden stool or box or sturdy chair, and lean over from the waist up, until my camera lens is directly over a stamp or cover lying flat on a contrasting-colored piece of paper or on the unprinted back cover of a clothbound book. Then I lower the camera by bending or stooping lower with my body until I can focus and "fill the frame" with just the stamp or cover dimensions, and I do this by adjusting the teleconverter and lens focus (outer) ring of the lens so that the philatelic gem becomes razor sharp.

Now the tricky part begins! Obviously a slight vertical motion either up or down with the camera will throw the whole image out of focus, so I brace my elbows on something (a pile of books, another lamp, whatever) and set the lens at a relatively high speed (1/250 second works well for me) and a compensating low f-stop number (wide diaphragm opening), so that my through-the-lens light metering system gives me a "shootable" reading. Then I take a few pictures to bracket my shots by assuming that some of them will come out a little blurry.

The whole secret in this hand-held stamp photography is to shoot at a fast speed to stop any hand motion of the camera, and to be ready to squeeze the shutter button smoothly but instantly when the most intricate detail of the stamp's design comes into focus as you are looking at it through the viewfinder window. Of course, some of your shots will be fuzzy, but many will be remarkably in focus, with all of the paper fibers or engraved ink lines as pretty as anything in an APS handbook.

As for lighting, I also use a very unconventional (and philatelically dangerous) source: natural sunlight! I set up and focus with light bulbs, then just at the moment I feel ready to shoot the picture I pull up the window shade and let the afternoon sun's rays pour in and onto the stamp or cover for only the few seconds it takes me to put my camera back into a hand-held position and trip the shutter. Sunlight is the most perfect and natural light and therefore makes outstanding color photos; the great danger, of course, is letting the sun shine too long and thereby damage your philatelic item. Dark colors, either on the stamps or on the background material, tend to absorb heat rapidly and can cause fragile paper to buckle and distort, especially if it is thin paper or a mint stamp with full gum, for example.

All of the stamp photos on the covers of my books have been taken with the above method — on the counter next to the sink of my apartment's kitchenette — with a large window facing the western sun's rays (afternoon sun in Los Angeles tends to have burned off the morning's haze and seems to give better picture color, in my opinion, than morning sunlight). But I don't recommend sunlight photography for the fainthearted or for unsteady hands, so a couple of normal incandescent desk lamps should provide adequate illumination if also combined with "skylight" (natural daylight coming through a window, *without* direct sun's rays). Also remember that prolonged exposure to sunlight will definitely fade the color of many stamp inks and cancels or handwritten cover addresses. I used to use extension tubes, but they tend to make small stamps out of focus along their perforations.

THE COPY STAND METHOD

The *copy stand method* is what professionals use for close-up flat subject (two dimensional) photography, and it is quite easy if you aren't intimidated by the equipment. In addition to a camera with close-up focusing ability, you need a copy stand or adjustable tripod (that can point the camera *down*). The camera lens must be parallel to the stamp or cover's surface or the image will be distorted. Also, any three dimensional irregularities (a "bent" stamp, folded cover) will be quite difficult to keep in focus throughout its surface.

The copy stand, for sale at any good photo shop, allows you to keep the camera perfectly still during shutter exposure, and a cheap cable release will further minimize camera motion. Of course, a large f-stop number (small diaphragm opening) like f/22 gives a long depth of field, i.e., more of a small range of distances will be in focus than would be with a small f-stop number (large diaphragm opening); *but* you sacrifice high shutter speed options (1/250 sec.) with a small lens opening. It is more crucial that the camera be as still as possible in moderate lighting conditions when using, for example, settings like f/22 with 1/60 sec. You don't want glare or camera exposure problems with excessively bright light, but a strong light source is needed for serious color stamp photography.

I don't like fluorescent light because it makes everything look pale and too "blue." Visible light rays (and invisible infrared, for that matter; that's why the lighted bulb feels hot) tend to be shifted toward the red end of the spectrum with incandescent bulbs, and most philatelists agree that incandescent light shows stamp shades better than fluorescent light. Stamp show exhibitions (and, unfortunately, all too often the bourse tables) use fluorescent light because it is cheap, although some studies have concluded that prolonged exposure to fluorescent light can fade philatelic items also. All light presents a danger to stamps, and old stamps with pristine original colors are best kept stored in darkness most of the time, which is one reason the Smithsonian Institution rotates its philatelic rarities on display in the Hall of Postal History and Philately.

EQUIPMENT COSTS

Costs for photographic gear vary from store to store and from brand to brand, so you have to shop around a little for the best merchandise at the best price to suit your needs. If you plan to shoot close-up pictures every week, you may want nice equipment. If you intend to use it twice a year, the cheapest setup may suffice. Depending on the brands you select, these are rough retail prices that you can expect to encounter:

(1) 35mm adjustable camera — $250-$400 for the basic body, 50-55mm/1.7 lens (or its approximate), and hard or soft camera carrying case with shoulder strap. Of course, if you seek the best Nikon or Leica gear, you'll need a four-figure camera budget.

(2) Macro Focusing Teleconverter — $80-$120, and make sure it is a *macro* and not just the normal teleconverter. *Or* you can buy a close-up lens (microlens) at somewhat greater expense for top quality optics. *Or* extension tubes.

(3) Copy stand — $100-$150, including two side lights. *Or* buy a cheaper stand and use your own lamps.

(4) Cable release — $25-$50. Get the cheapest one if it works well with your camera.

And then you'll need a variety of flat colored backgrounds on which to photograph your stamps: colored cardboard at least as large as a sheet of typing paper is excellent: black, white, red, and dark blue are good background colors to add contrast to your stamps and covers.

FILMS   I like Kodachrome 64 for color slides, ASA 100 Kodak color print film for small prints and color enlargements, and Kodak Plus-X (ASA 125) for black-and-white prints. There is no point in using fast film (high ASA values) for philatelic photography because you can shoot at a faster speed if necessary, and you want to minimize graininess in the pictures. The film manufacturers all say that their fast films aren't very grainy, but the slower film ASAs are universally accepted for rich color rendition and sharp detail, so why not stick with the best?

And yes, it does make a difference who develops and prints your film. I insist on *Kodak Processing* (now called "Kodalux") for consistency and reliability; I figure by now Kodak knows how to develop their own films as well as any other company. And I often have my *prints* done by a local specialty photo lab which prides itself on professional-quality results, and which can custom print according to my specification (special papers, more or less contrast, etc.). Super Color of Los Angeles charged me only $1 per print for publishable prints of stamps for my second book, and these prints had much better color than the prints I got from Kodak when I had the roll originally developed.

STORAGE OF   The care and protection of photographs and color slides is a lot
FINISHED PHOTOS   like the proper storage of rare stamps. Keep them away from heat, humidity, sunlight, and dust. A cool, dark cabinet away from kitchens and bathrooms is usually good. Store both prints and slides upright if possible to prevent them from sticking together or getting scratched by dust. Slides file nicely in projector trays or rectangular boxes made for slides — both for sale at your photo shop. Prints can be filed in plastic or wooden file boxes, in manila file folders in normal metal filing cabinets, or carefully tucked in photo albums that *don't* damage the prints with adhesives or plastic overlays.

And by all means, your best stamp photos should be enlarged, framed under non-reflective glass, and proudly displayed on the walls of your home! Or they may be used to enhance a philatelic exhibit if the show's rules allow photographs, or to illustrate an article submission to the philatelic press.

Chapter 14

Stamp Auctions

The agent for Arthur Hind outbid Maurice Burrus and the agent for Britain's King George V for the unique British Guiana 1¢ black-on-magenta of 1856 at the third Ferrary sale in 1922; the hammer price was $32,000 (converted from 1922 French francs), a serious sum for the time, and a record up to that moment for the auction realization of a postage stamp. Unless you are content to have an ordinary collection with mediocre stamps and covers, you also must resort to *auctions* to acquire elusive pieces — like the full pane of 36 of the 1924 Mount Everest Expedition local, with selvage all around and rich color, which this author recently purchased for $440 (including commission) from a George Alevizos auction. And what better way to sell for current market prices than at unreserved public auction?

Of course, we have to be selective: Not every auction house is good for every type of collection. Some companies (like Siegel's, Harmers, and Christie's) actively solicit great rarities *and* have a catalog mailing list and an advertising budget to match the quality of stamps they attract for sale. Other firms specialize — in British Commonwealth (Colonial Stamp Company), Asian material (George Alevizos and Michael Rogers), U.S. errors (Jacques C. Schiff, Jr.), quality U.S. and foreign in all price ranges (Superior), U.S. classic covers (Richard C. Frajola, Al Zimmerman), or a little of everything from large carton lots to investment material (Rasdale Stamp Company, Richard Wolffers, Inc.).

This chapter distills what I have learned from twenty years of buying and selling stamps at auction. Let's look at auction buying first.

AUCTION BUYING
Here are a couple of dozen tips for successful philatelic auction buying.

Start Small
Start small and work your way up in auction buying. Don't spend your life savings in the first auction you can find. Submit

a few trial bids at moderate prices for stamps that you need for your collection; if successful, study your acquisitions and maybe give that company a group of larger bids next time. If unsuccessful in securing lots, analyze the prices realized as to whether or not your bids were realistic, by comparing what prices similar material sells for with this auction company and others.

Cheaper Lots

Cheap lots are as obtainable as more costly items in many stamp auctions. In the 1970s I purchased at a half dozen different auction firms a number of nicely centered (design clear of perforations, sound used copies) Black Jacks at around $25 each, and a handsome Penny Black with wide margins (and undamaged!) for $20 — at smaller auction houses where the bidding wasn't stiff. Or should I have squandered $8000 for a "choice" mint Zeppelin set in 1980, only to watch its market value crash shortly after?

Auction buying isn't only for big budgets. It isn't *how much* you spend but *how well* you spend that makes you a sensible bidder. Luck helps and knowledge helps, so you must read virtually all of the catalogs that offer material you seek — to compare prices and take advantage of bargains when you bid in the right sale at the right time.

Bidding Increments

Play special attention to the company's policy on *bidding increments*. Do they award lots to mail bidders at a slight advance over the next highest bid? Or are you participating in a *mail sale* without floor action, where all lots sell for top dollar to the *highest bidder*?

Some strategy for mail bidding: Try to bid the "limit level" before a higher increment is required in the bidding rules. For example, bid $200 instead of $190 for a lot if the next increase over $200 would be $25 more, for a total bid of $225, plus 10% auction commission for a cost of $247.50 plus shipping . . . enough to discourage some bidders from topping your $200 bid if they can calculate what the next increment will cost them!

Time Your Mail Bids

Time your mail bids to arrive at an advantageous day. If earlier tie bids get preference over those received later, and you plan to bid high, then send in your bid immediately. If you suspect the company (especially mail sale firms) tells other bidders what their highest book bids are, then mail in your bids at the last moment, say three days before the auction date, so they can't reveal

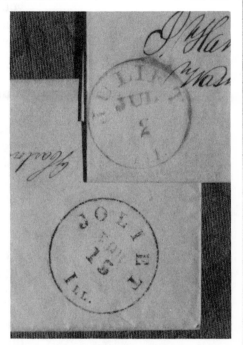

3¢ 1857 U.S. definitives tied to Joliet, IL covers. Stamp at left, cancelled July 22 (1859 — as per dated letter enclosed) is the 3¢ rose with top and bottom outer frame lines and is probably an illegally reused stamp, since other correspondence in this series shows the 3¢ stamp without horizontal frame lines, and because there is a suspicious amount of dried glue around the stamp which nevertheless seems to be properly tied. Stamp at right is variety without horizontal frame lines. From the author's collection of covers from the town of his birth, Joliet, Illinois.

Cancels on Joliet, IL stampless covers. The July cancel in red ink states "JULIET" which is what the town was first called in the 1830s. The Feb. 15 black postmark daters no later than 1845 when the name was changed to Joliet. Beware of adhesive stamps added to stampless covers to increase their value. Postmarks and other cover notations should all agree with the apparent time period in which the cover originated. Docketing inside the "Juliet" cover includes the date "1839."

Three copies of the 4¢ Trans-Mississippi issue of 1898 on registered cover from New Orleans, March 4, 1899 on 2¢ carmine on white embossed envelope. Cork killer cancels, nothing tied but probably authentic. The registry rate of that time of 10¢ plus either an overpaid or doubleweight letter (4¢) accounts for the total postage. No postal markings on the reverse.

your bids early. Also, if you are bidding in many different sales, it is nice to know what your auction bills are before you submit more bids to new sales.

Auction Rules Study the catalog auction rules for a company to which you've never submitted bills before. Familiarize yourself with the company's terms. (Does *unused* mean without gum? Does *mint* mean never hinged?) What abbreviations are used in catalog descriptions? What stamp catalog edition is being quoted? What do the auction catalog prices mean — current catalog value, retail value, estimated cash value (ECV), owner's estimated value, wholesale value?

Viewing of Lots Try to view auction lots before the sale date so you can leisurely study them, away from the pressure and noise of last minute crowds in the auction gallery. Ask permission to float a stamp in watermark fluid to check for repairs, and use the company's fluid and tongs. Always ask to touch a cover before you remove it from its protective plastic pocket. Ask before you examine an expensive stamp with tongs.

When I had a professional photographer take the pictures at Superior Stamp & Coin Company in Beverly Hills, California (for my book *Collecting Stamps for Pleasure & Profit*), Karl Hess of Superior's Stamp Department did all of the handling and positioning of the 24¢ Inverted Jenny copy from an upcoming Superior auction. Mr. Hass wisely wouldn't let the photographic crew touch this stamp, and when the camera started to slip on the copy stand just before they tripped the shutter, I prayed to Rowland Hill that the camera wouldn't fall and damage the $100,000 rarity — for which, of course, I was responsible because it was my photography project!

You can also view lots from certain companies by mail, paying insurance both ways, but I don't recommend this because it is risking getting a lot damaged or lost, to the annoyance of the company and potential bidders in spite of the fact that the lot is insured.

Add All Charges When Bidding Add all charges when mentally calculating your bids: the auction commission (usually 10% now that the 20% "American" rate is nearly obsolete), state sales tax, and shipping/insurance fees.

$100 is not the total price if you bid $100 on a lot. Add $10 commission, maybe 6% sales tax for another $6, and perhaps $5 or more for registered or insured mail if you're having it sent to your address, making a grand total of $121 (plus any check or money order fees and the stamps and stationery you used to correspond with the company).

Have heavy lots, like albums and large cover cartons, sent by cheaper means such as parcel post or the cheapest UPS rate. Air mail can be expensive when getting heavy packages from overseas. I don't even bid on cheap albums or bound philatelic literature in foreign auctions because the shipping costs would be prohibitive for air mail and surface conveyance is unreliable: An album took a month to go from London, England to Los Angeles by ship mail, and when I received it I noticed the package, though sturdily wrapped, appeared to have been fought over by a pack of dogs.

No "Buy" Bids   Never submit a "Buy" bid. Always put a specific amount of money in the bid sheet boxes, and for firms that offer it, enter a "limit" on the total amount of your bids so you don't exceed your budget in that sale.

Research Items   Do Your Homework before the auction. Research the rare and/or expensive items so you'll be an informed bidder. Don't take the catalog descriptions for granted; some companies consistently overgrade stamps, including both pictured and illustrated lots, and rarity and philatelic significance may be misstated. "Superb" and "Choice" are mental concepts, not indelible qualities of a stamp or cover. On the other hand, lack of time or knowledge at the auction house may result in "sleepers" slipping past the catalog describer, so an alert and informed bidder can still get bargains in late 20th century stamp auctions.

Request Photocopies   Request photocopies for lots that are not photographed in the catalog. Be suspicious of catalog description for unillustrated lots, especially regarding centering, margins, and perforation conditions. Some perforation teeth are uniform and clean in 19th century U.S. stamps, others are encountered with ragged appearance. I pass up as many stamps for perforation problems as I do for poor centering. Enclose a business-sized (No. 10) stamped, self-addressed envelope, plus another stamp or two in a small glassine, when requesting photocopies of lots. And record in your auction catalog that you're waiting for a photocopy so you don't send in your bids before you receive it.

Cash Deposits

Instead of sending a cash deposit as a first-time bidder, I always list my APS and Classics Society numbers, and sometimes another auction house where I've made recent purchases. Some of the big companies ask for cash deposits in lieu of strong references from new customers, but I have never had a bid sheet rejected because it lacked an accompanying cash deposit, which I think is an inconvenience for the customer.

If you're bidding for a $50,000 item, however, you can see why a well-run company may hesitate to execute your bid on the floor if you didn't send any references or deposit; it would alienate serious bidders contending for that lot if you won it and then failed to pay your bid promise. Bid sheets are *legal documents* and when signed constitute a binding contract between bidder and auction company should your bids be successful in the auction.

Small Companies Offer Bargains

Small auction companies have bargains in many of their sales because of limited customer competition. You could be the only person on their mailing list collecting Nyassa inverts (genuine, not the forgeries!), so when these stamps are offered as a lot you get them for a rock bottom price. I like to bid in mail sales from stable companies with full-page lot-listing ads in the philatelic weeklies, *after* I have sent for photocopies of the lots to verify the stamp centering. I have bought some beautiful used Canadian "Bluenose" copies as well as singles and used blocks of Canadian Jubilees in small mail sales. I get nervous about bidding and sending my money to *new* mail sales I have never seen before.

Bid More for True Rarity

Bid more generously if you have *never seen* the item offered for sale before. But you must study many different company auction catalogs to know if the material is indeed rare or merely infrequently handled by your favorite company. If it is in every sale, bid lower: Just because it is expensive doesn't mean you'll never see it again (U.S. Graf Zeppelins, routine copies of the 1847 first U.S. definitives, off-center $5 Columbians).

I've been reading all of the major U.S. auction company catalogs for twenty years, and now when I notice a stamp I've never seen auctioned before, I know it is truly rare.

Forms of Payment

When planning on participating in a floor auction, find out in advance what forms of payment are acceptable from floor bidders: cash, check, money order, credit card. I don't recommend paying bills on installment terms because I think, for peace of mind, stamp collecting should be done on a cash and carry basis. But if you seek installment terms for a precious lot that you can't instantly afford, ask the company *before* the sale if they will extend you installment credit. Or if you would rather see an auctioneer's face turn bright crimson red, publicly announce on the auction floor: "Gee, thanks for selling me $100,000 worth of Postmaster Provisionals. I'm broke today, but can I pay you $3000 a month?"

Control Your Emotions When Bidding

Electricity is in the air — three other bidders are determined to duel it out with you for the carton of Civil War patriotics. You have already exceeded your limit but you get excited and stay in the bidding battle until the auctioneer announces: "Sold to the customer with the hysterical bidding paddle. Six hundred dollars please, for a lot estimated at a hundred!"

Decide on your absolute *top bids* and write the amounts next to the lot numbers in the auction catalog, before live bidding frenzy distorts your better judgment. Ego wars and being a flashy spender on the auction floor may impress some of the spectators for a moment as you have your glory in the philatelic spotlight, but they're not the ones who will be *paying* the hammer prices of the lots that you win!

Sometime around 1970 or 1971 I fought another bidder in a Rasdale floor auction in Chicago — for a large cardboard box full of covers and miscellaneous junk on faded album leaves, and I won the lot for double the original limit I had pencilled in my auction catalog. At that same sale I dropped out of the action when a magnificent block-of-four of the 10¢ Registry stamp of 1911 reached $55, the cost of a moderately nice single of that stamp today. Such is hindsight in floor bidding experience.

It Is OK to Lose a Lot

Don't be afraid to walk away from an auction empty-handed, without winning any lots. There are stamp auctions every month. Why bid in this sale if the material isn't up to your standards or within your budget? Cash has value too — walk out the door with it instead of feeling as though you wasted your time by attending an auction where you didn't make purchases.

Bid on Several Lots at Floor Auctions

When attending a floor auction, go with more than one lot in mind if possible, so you won't be heartbroken if you are outbid on the first (or last!) lot in the sale, and then have nothing to look forward to. Alfred H. Caspary and Maurice Burrus personally attended the Ferrary sales as floor bidders in quest of spectacular specimens for their growing collections; and they didn't quit collecting because they didn't win every lot! If you have several collecting specialties represented in a floor auction, you'll enjoy your visit there more than if you nervously wait for the "one and only" important stamp to come up for bidding.

Bid Conservatively

The most enviable position to be in as an auction bidder is to desire some of the lots in a sale, but not want them so much that you feel you have to throw a great deal of money at them. Try bidding conservatively, both with floor and mail bids — say about 50% to 75% of the auction company's estimated hammer prices. You may be surprised how often you'll win such bids. Obscure specialist material in a small company's auction will sometime sell for much less than the identical items at Siegel's, Harmers, or Superior's. Of course if your collection needs a once-in-a-lifetime lot, then you have to up your bids.

Don't Be Intimidated at Floor Auctions

Don't be intimidated by an impressive auction gallery, the demeanor of the auctioneer, the other bidders in their fancy clothing, or by the high estimated cash value (ECV) of lots you are considering. Everybody has to start somewhere, and a cheap lot knocked down at a bargain price makes more sense than a costly lot sold for double its normal retail worth.

You're not in a movie script, you're at a stamp auction where *your* money and stamp collection are at stake. Bid what you think is reasonable for your budget. However, ridiculously small floor bids (5% to 10% of ECV) made seriously will probably annoy people who have not got time to waste.

Prepare Your Catalog Before the Sale

Make notations in the catalog as soon as it arrives in the mail. Circle lot numbers that interest you as soon as you read the descriptions. Write letters for additional information (How many millimeters is it torn? Is the back flap of the cover intact?) or send for photocopies immediately, and allow three or four days across the United States for mail in one direction. Write lot numbers on the catalog's cover so you can quickly locate them.

I like to print next to lot numbers the letters "OB" for *overbid* if I plan to bid more than the price listed in the catalog; or "UB" for *underbid* if I think the catalog-listed price is too high. Then, whether I'm a floor bidder or decide to send my bid sheet in at the last moment, I can quickly plan how I want to spend my money in this auction. Also, make notes for questions you want to investigate or ask the company's staff when you go to view specific lots on their premises.

Auction Agents

The use of auction agents is a personal choice. I prefer to inspect everything myself, but agents can help an advanced collector who can't attend a sale in person. Agents charge a fee, usually a percentage based on the prices realized of lots won for a client, and the bigger auction firms can recommend a reliable agent who frequents their sales. Obviously an agent shouldn't be hired to buy $20 lots because the commission has to be worth the agent's trouble.

Alfred F. Lichtenstein, Arthur Hind, and Britain's King George V were all represented by agents at the Ferrary sales in the 1920s. And George H. Worthington employed John N. Luff himself as an auction agent in New York. If you have to ask whether you need an auction agent, you probably do not.

Pay Auction Bills Promptly

Pay auction bills promptly (within a month, preferably on receipt) to maintain good credit ratings and a good reputation. Auction companies understand collector whims and cash flow problems, but if you are very late (several months) in paying your auction bills, you could endanger your reliability in the whole stamp trade because word gets around about "problem customers." Don't bid if you cannot afford to pay.

Study Prices Realized

Study prices realized when they arrive to evaluate how closely your bidding levels compare with actual hammer prices. Should you increase or decrease your bids for similar material in the next sale? What is the general price trend for items in your collecting specialty, in auctions over the past couple of years?

Full pane of 60 of Transvaal's 6-pence Queen Victoria issue of 1878. Scarce in full panes with no defects, the ½-penny through 2-shillings set of seven values is usually found off center, and individual stamps generally have damaged perforation teeth. Never bid on these unless you can see a photograph. Unillustrated lots of this set in British auction catalogs are invariably overgraded by American standards: superb used may actually be very good, off-center, ragged perfs, and disfiguringly cancelled.

Transvaal 1878 4-pence (three copies) on 1880 cover posted from Pretoria "via Kimberley" to England. Passed through Cape Town May 20 and arrived in Bristol on June 14, at Clevedon on June 15 as per backstamps. The letter rate to England at the time was 12 pence, and the three 4-pence adhesives properly paid the postage. Purchased by the author for $75 in 1974.

Save Useful Auction Catalogs	Save important catalogs as reference works for your personal philatelic library. Many specialized sales are permanent handbooks of lasting information value for your continuing research. Hardbound copies of "name sales" or annual runs of catalogs of big auction houses are available for purchase form literature dealers (see the end of Chapter 7).
Returning Lots	Return lots if you honestly believe them to have been seriously misdescribed, with unanticipated flaws, the wrong catalog numbers, poorly photographed, etc. Don't make a pest of yourself by returning lot after lot to a company if you want to stay on their mailing list.
	First-time bidders are always a little suspect, but are usually given the benefit of the doubt because firms want new customers. Return lots with a detailed note explaining your reasons, and most companies will honor your sincerity and do their best to resolve your complaints.
SELLING AT AUCTION	My experience has been that auctions tend to determine the true value of stamps, but you must carefully prepare the collection for sale, and select the appropriate auction house (see Chapter 7). My practice is to give a company a sample group of stamps or covers to auction off, wait until the sale is over, and then decide if I am pleased with the way they do business. Consign your best stamps to companies that earn the best prices and give you excellent service with cash advances, prompt payments after the sale, and accurate, positive catalog descriptions of your treasures.
Decide What to Sell	Save your best material for last and sell your second best. Keep your most memorable stamps — the ones with the highest market value, those that are hardest to replace, those that you still have an interest in studying. Sell the miscellaneous items you will never write up for competitive exhibition. Sell the choice material when you need money.
Get an Advance	Accumulate enough stamps or covers so you qualify for an auction advance, money forwarded to you on receipt of your consignment, to be debited against prices realized when your stuff is sold. Study what similar items are bringing when sold in that company's sales to estimate what your collection is worth to

them. Many companies will offer several hundred dollars advance on consignments of $1000 ECV.

Pick the Right Company

Choose the right company for your stamps. Small firms will more likely take cheap sets, seconds, large lots of cheap covers, and low total value consignments. Your great rarities (ECV over $1000 each) should go to the better auctions.

The largest auction firms have catalog mailing lists numbering thousands of active bidders. A new, unknown mail sale company will be lucky to get a few hundred bidders for a poorly advertised sale where even quality stamps may go begging for bids.

Arrange Your Collection for Sale

In arranging your collection for auction, make everything easy to examine. *No* sealed plastic mounts, *no* covers too securely mounted with adhesive corners. Clear-fronted plastic approval cards are better than opaque cardboard stock book sheets so the entire front of an item can be scanned without removing it. Mylar-type cover sleeves are good for protecting covers until the company transfers them to its own lotting sheet plastic pockets. List catalog values and other identifying data next to the better stamps. A damaged stamp in a set will make the auction company suspicious of the entire set. Group common material together, and separate rarities so auction company personnel can easily make up separate logical lots.

Be Patient

Be Patient! Auctions take enormous time, energy, and staff resources to prepare, conduct, and settle afterwards. I have often waited three to six months to see my money after sending my consignment to a company that holds monthly sales. The very next sale date may be already booked up, so you'll have to wait for a future sale, then another month or more after the auction date before you get your money. Remember, though, a cash advance can ease the waiting time.

No Reserves

I don't recommend placing reserves on your consignments. Do you want to sell or don't you? If your material is desirable and given to a famous company, chances are you will get a fair market price. If you are worried about receiving no serious bidders for a very specialized collection of unpopular stamps, then sell it outright to a dealer or by private treaty with a suitable dealer commission.

Chapter 15

Becoming a Stamp Dealer

Most stamp dealers started out as collectors. The accumulation of philatelic knowledge over the years, the love of the hobby, plus the appeal of making money doing what you are already doing for "fun" leads many a naive collector to thoughts of becoming a stamp dealer.

If you think you know more about stamps than the customers you intend to serve; *and* if you have another job or source of income or substantial cash savings; *and* if you can afford to operate your new stamp business at a loss for at least the first year or until your income exceeds your overhead; *and* if you are willing to work long hours that have no relation to the amount of money you are making; *and* if you already possess enough stamp or cover stock to attract customers; *and* if you have a detailed plan of action for starting your business, advertising, replacing stock, and handling unexpected emergencies, *then maybe* you are ready to try your hand at one of the most noble professions in the world; Philatelic Dealing.

EARLY STAMP DEALERS Jean-Baptiste Moens started selling stamps in his Brussels, Belgium bookshop at least as early as 1852. Edward Stanley Gibbons was born in 1840, the same year as the birth of the world's first postage stamp, Britain's Penny Black. He claimed to be a stamp dealer at age sixteen, and by 1874 he moved his store to London where it still exists as the oldest stamp company in the world. The Gibbons stamp catalogs are the oldest in continuous publication, begun by Gibbons himself in 1865.

And John Walter Scott became America's most well-known dealer after he came to the United States from England and began producing stamp catalogs in 1867 and 1868. Scott Publishing Company, now located in Sidney, Ohio, is a direct business descendant of J. Walter Scott's firm.

Ernest A. Kehr, in his book *The Romance of Stamp Collecting* (Thomas Y. Crowell Co., New York, NY, 1947, 1956), explained that stamp dealers in the late 19th and early 20th centuries lived in their shops, and many were ready and willing to share their knowledge and expertise with anyone who walked in. Two New York City dealers whom Kehr speaks fondly of were Percy G. Doane and John Murray Bartels.

And, of course, philately in America would be much poorer without H.E. Harris, Jacques Minkus, Herman Herst, Jr., Bernard Harmer, Robert A. Siegel, and Raymond H. and Roger G. Weill.

TYPES OF DEALERS

There are six main categories of *types of stamp dealers*, based on how their business is conducted. Of course some dealers may overlap into two or more categories, but most specialize in one of these types, which I discuss in order of increasing difficulty in operating.

Mail Order

Mail order dealers do their business by mail, buying and (especially) selling via ads, mailings, and price lists — with customers whom they may never meet and know only through postal correspondence. Many dealers start out as mail order businesspeople because they can work out of their homes, have minimal overhead, and can work part time until they are making enough money to quit their former jobs.

The advantages of mail order are: little capital and stamp stock needed (enough for your first classified ad!); you can do it while working another job or even going to school (I ran my first "stamps for sale" ad when I was a teenager); and you can work from the privacy and security of your home or post office box. Prime disadvantages of mail order are that collectors feel suspicious about ordering from or selling to a first time advertiser, and it may take a lot of advertising money to get "name recognition" among the collecting public.

Shows and Bourses

Renting a table or booth at *shows and bourses* gives you face-to-face access to many stamp enthusiasts. The bigger shows tend to draw more customers, and you also have the option of buying or selling with other dealers present. Bourse tables run from $50 to $400 or more for a typical society or club show, and you have to reserve them well in advance (the Long Beach, CA show is always sold out and has a waiting list). Also, watch out for signing up for a bourse that is being held on the same weekend as a competing show nearby. Most shows run for two or three days, e.g., Friday, Saturday, and Sunday.

Expenses can mount up ferociously when attending an out-of-town show as a dealer: air or surface transportation from your hometown, hotel costs, meals, and loss of work or business at your normal job if travel time eats into your regular work schedule (if you do stamp shows part time). It is easily possible to spend close to $1000 for all expenses to have a table at a major show, so you have to calculate whether your *profits* will compensate you for the show's overhead.

Advantages of show and bourse dealing are that you get to meet many new potential customers (whose addresses and want lists you can solicit); you compete more or less equally for business with other show dealers who offer the same material (at the same quality and price?); and since many stamp shows take place on weekends, you can do shows part time and not interfere too much with your other job. And if you do local shows with cheap table rent, the same customers tend to keep coming back and will get to trust you and give you their business.

The disadvantages of shows are that they can be time-consuming and costly if you have a small specialized stock with limited collector appeal; better stocked and better financed table holders may lure all of your business away; and it is possible at even the prestigious shows to get a poor customer turnout due to weather, location, competing shows on the same date, poor publicity, etc. (I once rented a table for four days at the APS Show in Anaheim and got little business because I was in the back of the hall and had limited stock appeal.)

Other show problems: Security may require that you deliver and pick up your stock at specified times and hall doors; this may be inconvenient for whatever reason. If you're a one-man operation, it is hard to leave your booth without losing potential business (as I did at the APS Show described above!), so you may have to have food delivered to your table and take hurried rest breaks. And more and more states are getting into the annoying habit of demanding sales tax records for stamp bourse sales, bureaucratic paperwork that drains some of your time and energy from the fun of doing a show.

Mail Sales   *Mail sales* (or mail bid sales, mail auctions) are lists of stamps by catalog numbers, printed either in an ad in the philatelic weeklies or on a direct mail flyer, to which your customers submit bids by a deadline date. Some prestigious auction houses began their firm's business by conducting mail sales. The difference between a mail sale and a floor auction is that there are no bidders present on a mail sale date.

You can more or less draw up your own rules for a mail sale, but ethics dictate that you cheerfully refund money for any reason at all if the bidder is dissatisfied with a won lot, *and* you must describe mail sale lots accurately to enhance your fledgling reputation and to avoid returned lots. If a lot isn't photographed, it must be well described according to standard auction terms, and be sure to mention any defects.

Some mail sale dealers have duplicate lots for some of their offerings, and accept bids at different amounts for the "same" lot number. Personal morals and long term ethics then come into play – do you give the slightly better stamp to the higher bidder, your best customer, or to a first-time customer to build your mailing list? Or do you reduce the higher bids and sell duplicate lots all at one price?

Mail sales are a lot of work. First you need plenty of stamps that customers are willing to bid on; then you have to write up the lot descriptions (or pay somebody to do it); then you have to advertise the sale and/or send a photocopied list to potential bidders (and where do you get their names in the first place?); then the work is only starting! You have to record, either in a computer or by longhand, all incoming bids at an advance over the last bid per lot; then you have to award lots to successful bidders and either mail them insured at once or send a notice for payment if you don't trust the bidder; then you have to process incoming payments (checks, money orders, credit cards if you are set up for them), send final lots out, deal with returns, and make some sense out of your customer list (whether to retain or delete a name, and why). For a thousand lot mail sale in a one-man operation, you've got plenty of hours cut out for you. And when this sale is all taken care of, it is time to start planning the next one.

Advantages of mail sales are: You can work from home at your own pace; you can start the business with lots from your own collection if it is substantial enough; you can reject any or all bids for a particular lot without giving any reasons why; and you can do it as a family operation or with limited paid outside help until (*and if*) the business booms.

Disadvantages of running mail sales are: Customers will definitely be leery of bidding in and sending money to a new mail sale dealer (no offense intended, but I never bid on a mail sale until I've seen it advertised a couple of times); the effort may not be worth the profits, especially if you have cheap lots going to many customers each (imagine a $4 lot to seventy-five different people!); and as a new dealer you may have trouble replacing the material that you sell from your own collection. (What do you do, offer "consignors" a commission? Buy outright? Why should they sell to a novice dealer?) And yet, many successful stamp dealers have run or are currently running mail sales, so if you are persistent there is some hope.

Retail Walk-In Shop   Now is probably a harder time than ever to open a *retail stamp store* due to the "soft" market, competition from other hobbies and leisure activities, and the sky-high costs of big city rent, taxes, insurance, etc. The small, dusty neighborhood stamp stores that dotted the landscape of America thirty years ago are rapidly becoming extinct, victims of urban "progress." Still, there is such a romance about the local stamp store, with its piles of albums, penny (or nickel) stamp boxes, and unusual covers and mint singles displayed under glass or on a bid board, that many a collector has daydreamed about one day opening and operating such a nostalgic philatelic realm.

It wouldn't hurt to get some real experience in stamp shop business by first working in one that is owned by somebody else, preferably one this is successful financially. And maybe even a store of the type that you personally aspire to own.

It has been said that location, location, and location are the three most important factors in the success of a retail store of any kind. I've visited over the past couple of years some beautiful stamp shops in the middle of nowhere, in some small town, or in a residential neighborhood that is hard to find, or on a second floor suite in a rundown business district with no parking and questionable security, whose proprietors complained to me about how bad stamp business is, and of how there is no future in it anymore. *On the same day*, mind you, I visited a thriving stamp retail store in a nearby city — a store in a nice business shopping mall with acres of free parking, well lit walkways, plenty of foot traffic, and a shop full of *paying customers* (certainly at much greater rent than the tacky places, but isn't location important?).

Luck, the proprietor's personality (can you get along with the curious public?), a decent stock of desirable stamps, and adequate capital play roles also in stamp store business. As I see it, a full service stamp shop (maybe combined with coins and a few baseball cards to get the kids inside) is the only way to go when deciding on retail store prospects. You must be prepared to *buy*

buy as well as *sell* to collectors, have a broad stock that appeals to almost anybody who walks in (*that* takes money), and you have to stock all the latest supplies so that customers can expect to buy whatever they need for their stamp hobby at one stop.

To put it bluntly, few people have the capital, time, stamp stock, knowledge, and congenial personality to become successful stamp store dealers from scratch. Now you may consider buying or leasing an established business intact, going into partnership with somebody (always difficult), or selling shares in your new store, but the odds for success are shaky unless you are still willing to work long hours day after day. But then there's nothing like being your own boss.

Some overhead expenses for the average stamp shop, which must be paid *before* any profits are drawn by the owners: building rent; utilities; property taxes if you own the premises; mortgage if you buy it; theft and fire insurance; advertising (if any!); store maintenance (cleaning supplies, brooms, etc.); other employee salaries (full or part time); burglar alarms and special locks and safes; any modification to the property necessary if it wasn't a stamp shop when you moved in; and, of course, enough stamp stock and supplies to attract customers off the sidewalk.

Do you think you could set up a wonderful store for less than $50,000? Some established dealers say that $50,000 would be cutting it a little thin! And in downtown New York or Chicago, that money wouldn't even pay the rent for a year unless your stamp shop was ten feet square, and maybe on the third floor.

But if you finally get the retail shop of your dreams, keep it organized. Everything should be on clean shelves or tables, sturdy countertops customers can lean on, everything in its place, easy to find, easy to sell. Keep expensive stamps and substantial cash locked up in a back room safe.

Public Auctions

There is something impressive and wonderful about seeing a full or half page display ad in the philatelic press announcing in quiet, understated terms that in two months a collection of great rarities will be "sold to order" at *public auction*. A floor auction differs from a mail sale in that there are live bidders present as well as mail bids on record. A numbered lot in public stamp auction is either knocked down to a book bidder who mailed or phoned his bid in, or is sold to a live floor bidder (who may not be so lively when he sees his total auction bill). And although it makes for bad public relations, lots in any auction can have a *reserve price* below which they won't be sold, such price being set either by the owner of the material or by the auctioneer; i.e., a responsible auction house won't let a valuable stamp sell "for a song," thereby protecting their consignors.

It is close to impossible to break into the stamp business with a public auction company unless you have enormous capital, good stamp stock of auctionable items, and a name that is already known among your prospective customers. More than one dealer has learned his trade by working as a lot describer and cataloger at a large auction company, then left and started his own auction firm. The stamp business may seem saturated with auction companies (several dozen at any given moment) but there is always room for somebody willing to work hard — excellence is rewarded in the stamp business as in other vocations. New companies spring up every decade to replace those that die.

So, assuming you *have been* in the stamp business for a number of years, have heavy capital reserves (maybe a $100,000 line of credit), and are willing to do friendly battle with the stamp auction firms already well established, then it is time to draw up a detailed plan for your auction company. Ask yourself these questions.

Why should people do business with me? What do I have to offer in the line of stamps, service, and personal attention to customer needs? Do I have enough employees to run an auction company? Where will the floor auction be held and how much will it cost to rent the hall, print and mail the catalogs, and advertise in the philatelic weeklies? How will I handle customer accounts — will I pay consignors immediately or only after payment by the bidders? What will I do with people who neglect to pay for lots won (and what will I do with those lots), and how do I determine who, if anyone, deserves auction credit? Can I get more stock for my next auction or will my sources of supply "dry up" if my first couple of sales rack up "low" prices realized?

Twenty percent payable by the buyer used to be the standard auction commission for stamp auctions in the U.S. Now almost every company has adopted the European practice of charging 10% to the seller, and 10% to the buyer. Will this commission pay for all of your overhead and leave enough cash left over for profit or capital business expansion? And if you auction your own material and receive unacceptably low bids on it, what do you do?

In the stamp auction business, as in few others, reputation is all important, and can be won or lost with equal ease. Collectors are nervous about consigning their expensive stamps to an untried new auctioneer, so the upstart auction firm has tremendous difficulty in obtaining desirable properties for auction. It isn't by chance that Siegel's and Harmers and Christie's and Superior get the best stamps for auction — they have reputations as big-time auctioneers, and consignors know the catalogs of these companies will reach serious, affluent bidders. So a new auction company almost always begins by selling cheaper material.

Wholesale   *Wholesale* is the hardest form of stamp dealing because you must please customers who are dealers, and why should they do business with you when they already have reliable sources of supply and good steady buyers? If, after some experience in the stamp business, you decide to dabble in wholesaling, you have to establish yourself as trustworthy and at least as professional as the other wholesalers.

What do you plan to wholesale? Supplies, covers, new issues, old issues, literature? Do you know where to pick up this material at prices allowing a profit when resold to dealers? And how do you know that dealers aren't going directly to these sources themselves?

More so about fifty years ago than today, certain dealers worked full time as "satcheleers," vest-pocket salesmen who made the rounds of stamp shops and bought and sold to their own accounts stamps that they recirculated among other dealers. Some of these vest-pocket dealers made money and had the advantage of no business overhead except for maybe carfare between stamp stores. Herman Herst, Jr. has often described these dealers who frequented the stamp shops in New York City when the stamp business was concentrated on Nassau Street in Lower Manhattan. A sharp knowledge of the current market value, some capital, and an in-depth knowledge of stamps are the minimum requirements for becoming a vest-pocket dealer. Would you like to volunteer?

Seriously, though, stamp dealing has rewards that go beyond mere money and business procedures. I've met dealers who regretted their professions, but I've met many who believe that stamp dealing was their heaven-sent calling, and they thank the day they chose to go into the stamp business. Carl Lipton, the Florida attorney who specializes in U.S. plate block dealing, says that just because you're in retail doesn't mean you're "dumb," and he told me the first time I met him that you tend to meet the nicest people in the stamp business, and that it is clean and respectable work. And Jay Tell of Americana Stamp and Coin Co. in Tarzana, CA went out of his way to emphasize to me, at our first meeting, that virtually all of his money is tied up in his stamp stock because he believes in and loves stamps, whether the market is up or down or momentarily uncertain. Mr. Tell explained very confidently to me that "We're in the stamp business for the long term," and his in-depth stock of U.S. issues backs up his words.

**DEALERS'
ORGANIZATIONS**

The two most prestigious stamp dealers' organizations are the ASDA and PTS. Write for application forms and current membership fees:

> American Stamp Dealers' Association
> 3 School Street
> Glen Cove, NY 11542
> (516) 759-7000
>
> Philatelic Trader's Society
> 27 John Adams Street
> London, WC2N 6HZ, England
> Telephone 01-930 6465

Membership in, and logo ad displays of, these organizations helps to inspire customer confidence in your business.

**THE STAMP
WHOLESALER**

The Stamp Wholesaler has been published continuously since it was founded in 1937 by the legendary Lucius Jackson, who wrote wonderful editorials before he passed away in 1978, using colorful language like: "I paid six Iron Men for that stamp . . . " (six $100 bills). Subscription rates are $20 per year for second class mailing (newspaper rate), $36 per year for surface mail to foreign countries. Published twenty-eight times a year, it has articles and ads to help the stamp dealer.

> *The Stamp Wholesaler*
> P.O. Box 706
> Albany, OR 97321
> (503) 928-3569

SUPPLIES DEALERS

These companies sell *stamp collecting supplies* (albums, books, mounts, tongs, etc.) at a discount to other dealers. Call or write for their latest price lists:

Brooklyn Gallery Coin & Stamp
8725 Fourth Avenue
P.O. Box 146
Brooklyn, NY 11209
(718) 745-5701

Discounted stamp supplies sold to anyone. Large classified ad every week in *Linn's*.

Cambridge-Essex Stamp Company
500 Eighth Avenue
New York, NY 10018
(212) 279-3724

Wholesale supplies to dealers only.

Harold Cohn & Company
3224 North Halsted Street
Chicago, IL 60657
(312) 472-0214

Wholesale supplies to dealers only; in Chicago for a long time. Remember buying HARCO brand stamp packets when you were a kid?

Global Stamp & Coin Company
460 Ridge Street
Lewiston, NY 14092
(716) 754-8513

Sells to anyone, all lines of supplies at discounts.

Lincoln Coin & Stamp Company
33 West Tupper
Buffalo, NY 14202
(716) 856-1884

Sells to anyone. Takes small orders also. I've been buying my Scott catalogs from them for years.

Mountain States Coin & Stamp Supplies, Inc.
8038 North 27th Avenue
Phoenix, AZ 85051
(602) 995-4497

Wholesale supplies to dealers only.

Pollard Coin & Stamp Supply Company
5220 East 23rd Street
Indianapolis, IN 46218
(317) 547-1306

Wholesale supplies to dealers only.

> Potomac Supplies
> 7720 Wisconsin Avenue
> Bethesda, MD 20814
> (301) 942-8300

Sells to anyone by mail, with customer discounts given. Has full page ads in *Linn's*.

> Subway Stamp Shop
> 111 Nassau Street
> New York, NY 10038
> (212) 227-8637

In business since 1931. Stocks all stamp supplies and offers discounts to anyone. Has a walk-in store and does occasional stamp shows. Full page ads in *Linn's*.

Chapter 16

Philatelic Writing

If you wait until you are a world-recognized expert in some branch of philately, or until you have acquired and exhibited a gold-medal collection, or until your writing ability is perfected, you may never get any stamp articles published. If you send a stamp article to a magazine, newspaper, or journal, the *worst* that can happen is that you will spend some time, effort, and a few cents worth of stationery and postage in preparing a short (three or four pages) manuscript for an editor's eyes — and learning a lot in the process, not only about stamps but also about how to submit an article for publication. The *best* that can happen is that your article will be published, you'll be paid for it, and you'll receive some fan mail from readers who enjoyed your writing.

If teenage "junior philatelists" and adult novice collectors can get an occasional piece published in the stamp weeklies, what are you waiting for? Even if you aren't a polished writer, editors will correct your grammar and word choice as long as your article is well thought out, neatly typed, and full of solid facts to the best of your knowledge.

I've had close to a thousand stamp articles published in the last twenty years, including my regular columns which have appeared in *Stamp Collector* and the *Los Angeles Times*, as well as free-lance pieces in *Linn's*, *Scott Stamp Monthly*, and specialist journals like the Illinois Postal History Society publications. Here are the steps I use when I write a stamp article for publication. If you follow what works for me you may have a very good chance of getting published.

PICK A TOPIC   Pick a topic that you think you can cover in an article. It must be something you have some knowledge of, for example: Great Britain postage dues, Viet Nam covers to the U.S. 1964-74, circus topicals (yes, some people collect topicals), hometown picture post cards that predate 1910, the Columbian Exposition commemoratives, U.S. air mail flat plate number blocks, World War

II patriotics, Confederate official envelopes, your favorite local stamp shop, your experience with stamp auctions, printing errors, your experience in competitive exhibiting, or pre-Union cancels on South African covers.

Make a detailed outline for your article. Rearrange the outline topics until they seem to be in a logical order, then use the outline to draft the article.

Select a title for your article that limits the scope of the subject (but editors will change titles anyway). Instead of "Italian Postmarks," how about "The Government Censor Markings and Postal Circular Datestamps on 1941-45 Covers from Rome." If you have collected and studied some philatelic specialty for a couple of years, chances are that you know a lot about it — that many other collectors may not know. Put it in a compact article.

A specialist society journal like *The American Revenuer* (American Revenue Association, 701 South First Avenue #332, Arcadia, CA 91006) or *The United States Specialist* (Bureau Issues Association, 834 Devonshire Way, Sunnyvale, CA 94087) will be read primarily by philatelists who are *already* informed about the basics in their field of collecting. *The Chronicle* (U.S. Philatelic Classics Society, 2030 Glenmont Avenue, N.W., Canton, OH 44708) doesn't need an article entitled "Why we should collect 19th century U.S. stamps" because virtually all of its readers already are deeply involved specialists in U.S. classic philately. They would rather see specific facts on specific stamps or covers, not general stamp collecting philosophy, which would find a better home in the pages of *Linn's Stamp News* or even in the monthly *The American Philatelist*.

PICK A MARKET

Pick a market for your article and write deliberately for that market. The three major stamp article markets are specialist and society journals, the general philatelic weeklies, and the general non-philatelic press, in order of increasing difficulty of getting the average stamp article published. Small stamp societies often jump for joy when they receive an unsolicited article for their journals, although they rarely pay anything because of tight budgets. A major big city newspaper (like *The New York Times* or the *Chicago Tribune*, which, by the way, published my first article when I was a teenager) is tough to break into, and that leaves the general philatelic press as target for your articles.

GENERAL STAMP PERIODICALS

The four prominent philatelic weeklies you should consider for a first-time stamp article are *Linn's*, *Stamp Collector*, *Stamps*, and *Mekeel's*. Just mail your article submissions or queries to "Editors" at these addresses:

> *Linn's Stamp News*
> P.O. Box 29
> Sidney, OH 45365
>
> *Stamp Collector*
> P.O. Box 10
> Albany, OR 97321
>
> *Stamps*
> 85 Canisteo Street
> Hornell, NY 14843
>
> *Mekeel's Weekly Stamp News*
> P.O. Box 5050
> White Plains, NY 10602

Scan the latest copies of your prospective publication to (1) see what *kinds* of articles they are publishing; (2) see what they *aren't* publishing; and (3) see their style of writing — every publication has its own idiosyncrasies of "in-house" style for punctuation, word choice, abbreviations, etc. (O.G. for "original gum," B.N.A. for "British North America"). An ideal article topic is one that the publication hasn't covered in a couple of years, but which you could shed new light on or update for the readers.

QUERY LETTER

A query letter outlining your proposed article is the professional way to introduce yourself and your writing ideas to an editor. Keep your letters to publishers short and confined to business. Limit query letters to one page; a couple of paragraphs is plenty! Editors are busy and aren't looking for a new pen pal every morning when they open their mail.

Also, it is considered pushy to bother an editor over the telephone. Let your query letter speak for itself, and *be patient* — give the editor time to consider your proposal. Wait at least one month before following up a query with a courteous note: "Have you had time to look over my query about French Foreign Legion mail . . .?"

Here is a sample query letter. Notice how short and to the point it is. Just give the information about your article that the editor needs to decide if the topic is needed for the publication.

```
1234 First Street
Anytown, U.S.A. 98765
December 29, 1990

Linn's Stamp News
P.O. Box 29
Sidney, OH 45365


Editors:

I am enclosing an outline of an article on Canadian revenue stamps that
I've been working up for publication. I've been collecting these stamps
for ten years.

May I send a completed article of approximately 600 words, plus three
black-and-white photos of stamps from my collection to illustrate the
text -- for your consideration for a future issue of Linn's?

Sincerely,


Hopeful Writer
```

WAITING FOR THE EDITOR'S DECISION

Waiting for a reply to your query can be nervewracking, but writing isn't for the impatient. Newspaper, magazine, and journal editors are busy, but they don't intentionally try to be mean to queasy first-time authors. If the editors like your article and believe it fits their periodical's publishing agenda, they will probably publish it when it is convenient for them.

But if they reject the piece, don't be heartbroken. Remember, *Gone With the Wind* was rejected by virtually every major publisher in New York when it was first submitted by Margaret Mitchell. If your article is rejected, consider sending it to another publication, but *don't* get angry with an editor for rejecting a piece. Editors have long memories, and someday you may want them to look at another piece of your writing. Remember, they are rejecting this particular *article*, they aren't condemning you personally, although authors do get emotionally tied up with their literary creations!

DECIDE ON LENGTH

If you are fortunate enough to get an editor's go-ahead for an article, or if you would rather just write it up first and submit it unsolicited on speculation ("on spec" in writer's slang), then you have to decide on the article's length. Will your piece be a couple of paragraphs explaining an interesting U.S. commemorative color-missing error, or will it be a full-length 3000 word photo-illustrated treatise on Norwegian postal stationery, complete with detailed footnotes and a descriptive bibliography?

If you double space an article, figure on about 200 words per page, leaving room for a one-inch margin all around the text. Drawings or photos of course take up space and have to be considered if page space is limited in the publication. What is the average length for an article similar to the type you are writing, in the publication for which you are writing it?

Cover your material clearly and concisely, but note that some editors like to receive more than enough words per article so they can cut back on what they don't like, leaving a tight, well expressed piece. So use your judgment as to length; cover the subject but don't waste words.

USE THE STYLE OF THE PUBLICATION

Style of writing varies from author to author and from publication to publication. Try to write using the periodical's general style so the editor will feel comfortable reading it and including it in an upcoming issue. Check and compare your article with material already published in your prospective periodical: average paragraph size, sentence length, word choice, abbreviations, and degree of writing formality.

In general, daily city newspapers use shorter paragraphs than specialist magazines like *National Geographic*. Editors will adjust your writing style as best they can to conform to what readers have come to expect in their publications, but you are more likely to get published if you somewhat "imitate" the typical in-house style in your entire article, without destroying your own personality which, if you can display it in your writing, is always a key to good authorship.

REVISE THE ARTICLE

Revise the article by letting it sit for a few days, and then go back and reread it to correct mistakes in information or spelling/ grammar, poor word choice, and redundancy or lack of clarity. I can type a nice article on the very first copy, with little to revise or proofread, but that is because I've been writing for publication for a long time. When you're starting out as a new stamp writer, even doing a "one-shot" piece describing the joys and wonders of your favorite stamp shop, you can't afford the lazy luxury of thinking that you're better than Shakespeare on your first draft!

Think about your target audience as you write. Pretend they are in the room with you and you are explaining your Austrian semi-postals to them, but instead of speaking the words, type them. Beginning writers tend to be too formal and stiff in their styles; just say what you want to say in simple words, and *don't* keep revising until it is perfect. Your article, like a stamp collection itself, will never be perfect, so send it off when you believe it is a good piece of work, representing your honest thoughts and efforts about an intriguing aspect of philately.

ILLUSTRATIONS

Illustrative drawings, charts, photographs, or color slides will impress editors if such material accompanies your article. Pack photos and slides well with strong cardboard so nothing gets bent en route. And don't send your only copy of an impossible to replace slide or photo negative unless you are willing to risk losing it in transit. Send one top quality photo rather than a dozen out of focus ones. You might inquire first whether the editor prefers slides (as many slick paper magazines) or black-and-white prints (as many newspapers do). See Chapter 13 for photographing your collection.

Usually if the article is about general philately or opinions on catalog value, prices, the Postal Service, etc., photo illustrations aren't essential. If you're writing about specific stamps or covers, illustrations may be mandatory. And some editors may have stock photos already on hand which they can use with your article (the U.S. Zeppelin stamps, Penny Blacks, famous inverts).

REFERENCES

Cite a few references for more scholarly articles, either within the body of the text or as a footnote/bibliography section at the end. References show that you aren't taking questionable technical/historical information merely out of your own head.

Public libraries and philatelic libraries (see Chapter 10) have stamp books that you may not possess in your home library. Local stamp shops and university libraries can supply some reference material. And don't forget back issues of stamp periodicals, either the original paper copies or microfilm on file in general public or specialist philatelic libraries (remember the *Society of Philatelic Americans Journal*?).

But be certain your references are timely. Many older stamp

books are in error because later research has corrected their mistakes.

SENDING THE ARTICLE

At last you're ready to send the article to the publisher. Is it neatly double-spaced on clean white typing paper? Do you have carbons or photocopies of all pages in case the submission gets lost in transit? Do you have a cardboard manuscript mailing box or 11 x 13 inch strong manila envelopes with cardboard inserts to protect both sides of the *unfolded* pages? Is your cover letter attached, with a business-sized (No. 10) stamped addressed return envelope for the editor's convenience in replying?

Then seal your masterpiece with mailing tape, properly address it with clear typing or hand printing, and affix real postage stamps to cover the cost of mailing. I believe in using the Postal Service to carry a stamp article to a new editor — stamps are the best ambassadors for themselves, and most likely the publication's editor is a stamp collector who will appreciate and wonder at the impressive appearance of a well put together parcel franked with obsolete U.S. commemoratives neatly lined up in the upper right corner above the addressee's name.

ONE PUBLISHER AT A TIME

It is considered unethical for a writer to send the same article to different publishers *without* letting all of them know that other editors are also seeing it. Editors don't have time to waste on submissions that they aren't likely to earn due to games being played by an unreliable writer who submits to many publisher in the hope of accepting the "best offer." I also don't recommend duplicate queries for beginning writers of stamp articles; the stamp periodical market is small enough that you can wait a month for each editor to respond to your query in sequence. *One publisher at a time!* For addresses of specialist societies, consult *Linn's Stamp World Almanac* (listed in the Bibliography of this book).

KEEPING RECORDS

Keeping records on your article queries and submissions can be done with a file box and index cards, filing cabinet for 8½ x 11 manila folders, or the equivalent on a home computer. you will need to refresh your memory about publications to which you have written, a list of article titles sent, the dates sent, and the dates when replies are received, as well as what the editors said in their letters.

Your records must be up to date on any payments received in compensation for your writing, in case the IRS or anybody else needs to know your income from publishing articles. Remember that most stamp specialist society publications offer no payment at all for articles; writing for them benefits the membership which contributes yearly dues that rarely allow surplus funds to be budgeted for article payment for pieces appearing in the society's journals and newsletters.

The greatest reward any writer can get is the knowledge that the published written word confers a kind of immortality on its author. We write so that other human beings can share our opinions, our thoughts, and our hard-acquired knowledge.

Stamp collecting is the hobby of kings and queens. What is your favorite aspect of philately? And isn't it time that you wrote an article about it?

Bibliography

Here are some of the better stamp books ever written. I have listed those that I *didn't* mention in my last book (*Stamp Collecting*, Betterway, 1989) to avoid duplicate information. This list is *representative*, not comprehensive, of good philatelic literature, even when added to the titles cited in my previous book.

Many are out of print, but can be ordered as used copies from philatelic literature dealers such as:

Leonard H. Hartmann
P.O. Box 36006
Louisville, KY 40233
(502) 451-0317

Empire Group
P.O. Box 2529
West Lawn, PA 19609
(215) 678-5000

David G. Phillips Company, Inc.
P.O. Box 611388
North Miami, FL 33161
(305) 895-0470

American Air Mail Society. *American Air Mail Catalogue*. Volume One, Fifth Edition, The American Air Mail Society, Washington, DC, 1974. Considered the standard reference on air mail covers. Vol. 1 discusses U.S. Pioneer and Governmental flights, Army and early foreign flights, Siege of Paris Balloon Posts, world Zeppelin covers (priceless information), crash covers, Philippine flights, and Propaganda Leaflets. 474 pages plus several blank for notes, clothbound. Currently sold by literature dealers for $12.50 (what a bargain!). Illustrated. Volumes 2 through 5 cover things like Domestic Air Mail Rates, Airport Dedication Covers, Canada, and Helicopter Flights. All currently available.

Amick, George. *The Inverted Jenny: Mystery, Money, Mania*. Amos Press, Sidney, OH, 1986. A 250-page illustrated story book of facts and tales behind the famous 24¢ air mail invert. Of special interest is the Appendix giving the known history of each plate position of this stamp in recorded transactions since Col. Green owned the pane, and a valuable list of references. $19.95 currently.

Antrim, E. *Civil War Prisons and Their Covers*. Collectors Club, New York, NY, 1961. Useful for attributing and analyzing Civil War POW mail from Northern and Southern prisons. 215 pages. $35.

Baker, Hugh J. and Baker, J. David. *Baker's U.S. Classics*. U.S. Philatelic Classics Society, Columbus, OH, 1985. 343 pages illustrated with black-and-white postmark drawings and cover photos. A compilation of their column about U.S. classic stamps and covers, which appeared in *Stamps* magazine from 1962-69. Useful in conjunction with such references as *Sloane's Column* by G. T. Turner, *Pat Paragraphs* by Elliot Perry, and *Ashbrook Special Service* by Stanley Ashbrook. $32.50 current. Clothbound.

Berthold, Dr. Victor M. *Handbook of the Wells, Fargo & Co.'s Handstamps and Franks used in the United States and Dominion of Canada and Foreign Countries*. Scott Stamp & Coin Co., New York, NY, 1926. Reprinted several times. 85 paperbound pages of precious information on the celebrated Wells, Fargo & Co. covers of the 19th century. $10-$20 used.

Bierman, Stanley M. *The World's Greatest Stamp Collectors*. Frederick Fell Publishers, New York, NY, 1981. 296 pages hardbound. Dr. Bierman is a practicing dermatologist in Los Angeles, and has one of the finest private philatelic libraries in the world. I've heard him lecture on dermatology at UCLA's School of Medicine and was deeply impressed with his technical expertise and command of the English language. A serious scholar of 20th century stamp collectors. $20 used.

Boggs, Winthrop S. *Postage Stamps and Postal History of Canada*. 2 Volumes. Chambers Publishing Co., Kalamazoo, MI, 1946. The first and most complete edition, later shortened and reprinted by Quarterman, 1975. Still the standard Canadian stamp reference. Original edition $100-$225 used. Reprint $60-$75. 825 original pages, cloth.

Cole, Maurice F. *The Black Jacks of 1863-1867*. Chambers Publishing Co., Kalamazoo, MI, 1950. 121 paperbound pages. Forerunner of Lane's book. Getting scarcer. $50 used.

Frickstad, Walter N. *A Century of California Post Offices, 1848-1954*. Philatelic Research Society, Oakland, CA, 1955. 395 paperbound pages; has been reprinted. A basic state post office reference. Consult a literature dealer for other states. $30-$40 used.

Speaking of California, this book goes well with other classic references like *Letters of Gold* by Coburn, *The Gold Rush Mail Agents to California* by Wierenga, *Gold Rush Steamers of the Pacific* by Wiltsee, etc.

Glass, Sol, *United States Postage Stamps: 1945-1952*. Bureau Issues Association, West Somerville, MA, 1954. Beautiful illustrated treatment of mid-20th century U.S. stamps and their backgrounds, including photos of rejected designs (fascinating!), printing plate statistics, and what actually happened at each first day ceremony. At the time of publication, Mr. Glass was BIA President, and he generously donated all rights and profits from this book to the BIA. Hardbound. $25 used.

Gobie, Henry M. *U.S. Parcel Post: A Postal History*. Postal Publications, Miami, FL, 1979. A definitive study of the first U.S. Parcel Post system and the 1913 stamps associated with it. Would be difficult to write a better book of similar length on the same subject. This is the format you want to use if you are writing a long treatise covering all essential aspects of a stamp series. Hardbound. $25-$30 used. Gobie also wrote the *Special Delivery* book.

Hargest, George E. *History of Letter Post Communication Between the United States and Europe 1845-1875*. Quarterman Publications, Lawrence, MA, 1975 reprint (first published 1971). 234 original hardbound pages. Discusses postal rates and routes of trans-Atlantic mail of this time period. $35-$50 used.

Hodder, Michael J. and Bowers, Q. David. *The Standard Catalogue of Encased Postage Stamps*. Bowers and Merena Galleries, Wolfeboro, NH, 1989. A desperately needed 191-page thoroughly illustrated paperback book on the varieties of U.S. encased postage stamps (other countries have issued them also). Comments on relative scarcity and prices these items in grades Fine through Uncirculated (numismatic terms). And, as in any in-depth treatise, *please* be careful and charitable when reading typographical errors which could confuse the novice, such as on page 98 where the 1¢ Drake's Plantation Bitters is quoted at $450 AU, but only $400 Unc. This book is $19.95 currently.

Lane, Maryette B. *The Harry F. Allen Collection of Black Jacks*. The American Philatelic Society, State College, PA, 1969. 148 hardbound pages, with emphasis on cancels and usages. Extension of Cole's work. $60-$95 used.

Linn's Staff. *Linn's World Stamp Almanac*. Fifth edition, Amos Press, Sidney, OH, 1989. Since the first edition in 1977, this paperback has been an invaluable reference for the stamp collector. 994 pages of small print at $19.95 is money well spent. Everything from facts on U.S. mail service to discussions of exhibiting and stamp auctions.

Lowe, Robson (Publishers). *The Encyclopedia of the British Empire* (Billig's Philatelic Handbooks). Robson Lowe Ltd., London, England, 1948. 5 volumes of the Empire in Africa and Australasia. Get the volume for the country of your specialty. Reprinted many times, these profusely illustrated books explain much postal history. $25 per volume. Hardbound.

MacBride, Van Dyk. *Confederate Patriotic Covers*. American Philatelic Society, State College, PA, 1943. Reprinted by Triad Publications, Weston, MA, 1979. 64 paperbound illustrated pages of Confederate patriotics. Mentions comparative rarity of cover designs. $25-$35. One of many companion treatises to go with Dietz references.

Neinken, Mortimer L. *The United States Ten Cent Stamps of 1855-59*. Collectors Club, New York, NY, 1960. 252 pages clothbound; a basic reference work by the author of similar volumes on the 1¢ stamp of 1851-61 and 12¢ issue of 1851-57. $30-$45 used.

Remerle, C.W. *U.S. Railroad Postmarks 1837-1861*. American Philatelic Society, State College, PA, 1958. 169 illustrated pages; the standard reference for this time period. Hardbound. $125-$225 used. Companion reference for Towle and Meyer's 1861-86 study.

Schmid, Paul W. *How to Detect Damaged, Altered, and Repaired Stamps*. Palm Press, Huntington, NY, 1979. Other references exist on stamp repairs, but this 105-page hardbound book presents the *minimum* knowledge needed by a wary philatelist. Chapters on gum, perforations, design alterations, etc. $17.50.

Skinner, Hubert C. and Eno, Amos. *United States Cancellations 1845-1869*. American Philatelic Society, State College, PA, 1980. An extension of the Herst-Sampson volume of fancy cancels. 363 thoroughly illustrated pages with careful drawings of 19th century U.S. cancels listed by types (Geometrics, Flags, Masonics, etc.) and attributed to specific towns where known (priceless information), and earliest year of use (by stamp issue). Hardbound, out of print. $50 used.

Stanley Gibbons Publications. *Stanley Gibbons Great Britain Specialised Stamp Catalogue, Volume 1: Queen Victoria*. Stanley Gibbons Publications, London, England, 1985. A lifetime of study in 404 compact pages. In-depth detail on 19th century Great Britain stamps. Hardbound. Vol. 2 covers Edward VII to George VI. Vol. 3 has pre-decimal Elizabeth II. Vol. 4 has decimal issues of Elizabeth II. I picked up my copy at a literature booth at AMERIPEX in Chicago in 1986. For the connoisseur of Great Britain.

Toppan, Deats, and Holland. *Historical Reference List of the Revenue Stamps of the United States* (Boston Revenue Book). Quarterman Publications, Lawrence, MA, 1980 reprint of 1899 original. 423 pages of early U.S. revenue information. Clothbound. $100 used.

Van Dam, Theo. (editor). *The Postal History of the AEF, 1917-1923*. American Philatelic Society, State College, PA, 1980. 242 hardbound pages compiled by the World War I Study Group of the War Cover Club. Chapters are signed by each author. Impressive scholarship of WWI philately. $20 used.

Williams. L.N. and Williams, M. *Rare Stamps*. G.P. Putnam's Sons, New York, NY, 1967 (printed in Germany). 120 pages, hardbound, of color and black-and-white photos of some of the world's rarest stamps, with stories about them. An inspiring book of classic rarities, good bedtime reading for those who admire the rare and the beautiful. These British authors have been writing about stamps since 1934 and their knowledge is formidable. Out of print but in many public libraries. $12.50 used. And if you think these authors are superficial, see their *Fundamentals of Philately*, 1971; 629 pages presenting a graduate course in stamp manufacturing.

STAMP RECORD					
Collection Item# ➡	408				
Country	Spain				
Cat.#	Unlisted				
Cat. used					
Cat. value at time of purchase					
Item Description	1930s Span. Civil War, local grn. on Wh., perf. 11x12				
Postal State	✳ 田				
Condition	F-VF Cent. 2 mm. UL corner crs.				
Price Pd. in U.S. $	$35.00				
Date Purchased	8-4-91				
Where Purchased	Brosius Stamp & Coin, Santa Moni-Ca.				
Other Remarks	One of three blocks known, acc. to Smith. Poss. Andalusia.				

STAMP RECORD					
Collection Item# ➡					
Country					
Cat.#					
Cat. used					
Cat. value at time of purchase					
Item Description					
Postal State					
Condition					
Price Pd. in U.S. $					
Date Purchased					
Where Purchased					
Other Remarks					

STAMP RECORD

Collection Item# →					
Country					
Cat.#					
Cat. used					
Cat. value at time of purchase					
Item Description					
Postal State					
Condition					
Price Pd. in U.S. $					
Date Purchased					
Where Purchased					
Other Remarks					

STAMP RECORD

Collection Item# →					
Country					
Cat.#					
Cat. used					
Cat. value at time of purchase					
Item Description					
Postal State					
Condition					
Price Pd. in U.S. $					
Date Purchased					
Where Purchased					
Other Remarks					

STAMP RECORD

Collection Item# →					
Country					
Cat.#					
Cat. used					
Cat. value at time of purchase					
Item Description					
Postal State					
Condition					
Price Pd. in U.S. $					
Date Purchased					
Where Purchased					
Other Remarks					

STAMP RECORD

Collection Item# →					
Country					
Cat.#					
Cat. used					
Cat. value at time of purchase					
Item Description					
Postal State					
Condition					
Price Pd. in U.S. $					
Date Purchased					
Where Purchased					
Other Remarks					

STAMP RECORD

Collection Item# ➡					
Country					
Cat.#					
Cat. used					
Cat. value at time of purchase					
Item Description					
Postal State					
Condition					
Price Pd. in U.S. $					
Date Purchased					
Where Purchased					
Other Remarks					

STAMP RECORD

Collection Item# ➡					
Country					
Cat.#					
Cat. used					
Cat. value at time of purchase					
Item Description					
Postal State					
Condition					
Price Pd. in U.S. $					
Date Purchased					
Where Purchased					
Other Remarks					

STAMP RECORD					
Collection Item# ➡					
Country					
Cat.#					
Cat. used					
Cat. value at time of purchase					
Item Description					
Postal State					
Condition					
Price Pd. in U.S. $					
Date Purchased					
Where Purchased					
Other Remarks					

STAMP RECORD					
Collection Item# ➡					
Country					
Cat.#					
Cat. used					
Cat. value at time of purchase					
Item Description					
Postal State					
Condition					
Price Pd. in U.S. $					
Date Purchased					
Where Purchased					
Other Remarks					

STAMP RECORD					
Collection Item# →					
Country					
Cat.#					
Cat. used					
Cat. value at time of purchase					
Item Description					
Postal State					
Condition					
Price Pd. in U.S. $					
Date Purchased					
Where Purchased					
Other Remarks					

STAMP RECORD					
Collection Item# →					
Country					
Cat.#					
Cat. used					
Cat. value at time of purchase					
Item Description					
Postal State					
Condition					
Price Pd. in U.S. $					
Date Purchased					
Where Purchased					
Other Remarks					

STAMP RECORD					
Collection Item# →					
Country					
Cat.#					
Cat. used					
Cat. value at time of purchase					
Item Description					
Postal State					
Condition					
Price Pd. in U.S. $					
Date Purchased					
Where Purchased					
Other Remarks					

STAMP RECORD					
Collection Item# →					
Country					
Cat.#					
Cat. used					
Cat. value at time of purchase					
Item Description					
Postal State					
Condition					
Price Pd. in U.S. $					
Date Purchased					
Where Purchased					
Other Remarks					

STAMP RECORD					
Collection Item# ➡					
Country					
Cat.#					
Cat. used					
Cat. value at time of purchase					
Item Description					
Postal State					
Condition					
Price Pd. in U.S. $					
Date Purchased					
Where Purchased					
Other Remarks					

STAMP RECORD					
Collection Item# ➡					
Country					
Cat.#					
Cat. used					
Cat. value at time of purchase					
Item Description					
Postal State					
Condition					
Price Pd. in U.S. $					
Date Purchased					
Where Purchased					
Other Remarks					

STAMP RECORD					
Collection Item# ➡					
Country					
Cat.#					
Cat. used					
Cat. value at time of purchase					
Item Description					
Postal State					
Condition					
Price Pd. in U.S. $					
Date Purchased					
Where Purchased					
Other Remarks					

STAMP RECORD					
Collection Item# ➡					
Country					
Cat.#					
Cat. used					
Cat. value at time of purchase					
Item Description					
Postal State					
Condition					
Price Pd. in U.S. $					
Date Purchased					
Where Purchased					
Other Remarks					

STAMP RECORD					
Collection Item# ➡					
Country					
Cat.#					
Cat. used					
Cat. value at time of purchase					
Item Description					
Postal State					
Condition					
Price Pd. in U.S. $					
Date Purchased					
Where Purchased					
Other Remarks					

STAMP RECORD					
Collection Item# ➡					
Country					
Cat.#					
Cat. used					
Cat. value at time of purchase					
Item Description					
Postal State					
Condition					
Price Pd. in U.S. $					
Date Purchased					
Where Purchased					
Other Remarks					

Index